To my best boy.

May the wonders never cease.

"So, do you actually know this guy you're taking off with?"

Jaime looked at me through the rearview mirror. His eyes were hidden behind his dark sunglasses, but I could tell he was teasing. The "guy" I was taking off with was his old college roommate, Jeff, who was sitting right next to him in the front passenger seat of the Volvo station wagon. The three of us were winding through the cement maze of Houston morning traffic on the way to George Bush Intercontinental Airport, where Jeff and I were scheduled for a flight.

"Jaime, *no*," said Jeff. He said it with a half smile, like a reprimanding mother trying to hide her amusement over a childish misdeed.

"Just saying," continued Jaime, "that as one of the few people who's had the 'pleasure' of travelling abroad with you, I think she deserves to know what she's getting into." He took a hand off the steering wheel, grinned, elbowed Jeff, and then returned to my reflection in the rearview mirror, waiting for an answer. *Do you actually know this guy?*

I didn't know how to answer the question. I evaded instead. "Is there anything I *should* know?"

"How many hours do you have?" joked Jaime. "I bet he 'forgot' to mention the time he ripped the saline IV out of his arm and jail-broke out of that hospital in Paris. It was the morning after Bastille Day. Jesus, he was running down the hallway in one of those little paper gowns. You know—the kind where you can see the ass? Didn't even stop to put on clothes, just barreled out the door and booked it right out of France."

"Jaime, *no!*" yelled Jeff, with pretend horror. "That was twenty years ago. Our balls had barely dropped."

"I don't know, man," said Jaime, shrugging his shoulders, "Let's just say my rosary is going to get a workout during the next three weeks."

I sat in the backseat, running my fingers along the embroidered hem of my dress. Out towards the horizon, past the half-built subdivisions and empty cement lots, I could see a line of tiny planes lifting off into the smoggy morning sunrise. We were getting close. In a few hours my plane—our plane—

would be taxiing onto the runway. It was a fair question: did I actually know the man who would be sitting beside me as the wheels lifted off the tarmac?

Yes. And no.

I knew Jeff was a science professor and a sixth-generation Texan with a wild glint in his eye. I knew I'd thought, "Oh, *you* again," when I met him for the first time, like I'd just bumped into an old friend. I knew our relationship had escalated into a flashing, tilt-a-whirl circus after a single round of tequila. I knew he liked chocolate with flecks of sea salt. I knew that he'd been married six years and separated for two, that he had a five-year-old daughter with bright, brown eyes, and that he chased the unconventional life like a migratory bird flying north for winter instead of south. I knew he was a sparkling provocateur, but Tupac's "Dear Mama" made him cry and he occasionally stopped the car to gently lift dead cats from the road and deposit them under bushes—a tender-hearted joker, if there was such a thing.

But did I truly know him? I had no earthly idea. How well can you know someone you just met online?

Maybe time and circumstance didn't matter so much in this story. In the handful of weeks since our first irreverent online dating emails—batted back and forth like tennis balls—Jeff had managed to penetrate my formidable wall of reserve. A rare feat. After a week, I agreed to meet him in person. Our first date was more like a reunion than an introduction.

Given our stark differences, the connection was surprising. I spent the first thirteen years of my life in rainy Portland, Oregon. There were seven of us: my parents, my three sisters, my brother, and me. We lived in a 100-year-old, one-bathroom Victorian house on Tillamook Street, named after an indigenous tribe in the Pacific Northwest. My parents chose to homeschool us, partially out of concern over our quality of education and partially out of a deep religious conviction. (I genuinely imagined the local middle school as a den of iniquity littered with condoms and needles.) My mother was devout, but she ensured that all five of us were well educated and socially competent. We bore no resemblance to the breed of Christian homeschoolers who were clad in long skirts and denim and forbidden to date or dance. The summer that the Twin Towers fell, we moved to Fort Worth, Texas. I came of age in Cowtown, where a storm could turn the sky boiled spinach green and snakes rattled in the grass. People loved football (almost) as much as Jesus.

In contrast, Jeff had always been a Texas boy. He and

his three sisters grew up four hours to the south in Houston and San Antonio. He spent summers fishing and hunting for Apache arrowheads on the Hill Country farm where his great-great- grandparents built a split log cabin. In college, during his more conservative days at Texas A&M, he was a card-carrying, tobacco-chewing Young Republican who could tear up the country dance floor.

His personality was like Texas. Larger than life. As a kid, he confided to his doctor that his secret fear was not tarantulas or kidnappers, but spontaneous combustion (like the drummer from *Spinal Tap* who vanished in a cloud of smoke after a particularly epic drum solo). He was a live conduit, electrifying to everyone he met. (And he'd met a lot of people.) He delighted in sudden intimacy, adventure, spectacle, and flashy coloured prints.

Subtle was not in Jeff's vocabulary, though it was a go-to in mine. All members of my family were dyed-in-the-wool introverts (myself included). If he was the torrid, restless *yang*, I was sensitive, introspective *yin*. For every pair of Jeff's brightly shaded chinos and lightning-spangled socks, I had a cardigan in heather-gray or cream. My houseplant-to-friend ratio was 10 to 1. I could happily go an entire day without uttering a syllable.

A few weeks into our nascent romance, we took a personality test confirming my suspicion that we had diametrically opposed personality types: he was an alpha go-getter who could charm a gate off its hinges while I was a quiet dreamer who could listen to all thirty-three hours of James Michener's *Poland* on cassette tape without dozing off.

At times, people mistakenly interpret my introversion as haughtiness. But Jeff was different. From the first date he made it clear that he was in holy awe of my capacity to sit still and reflect. He treated my penchant for silence as one might treat an alien species under careful observation.

"Just curious. How many words did you speak out loud today?" he asked a week after we met. We were sipping pints in a dim Austin bar.

"Before this beer? I guess I ordered a coffee from the barista this morning," I said, counting on my fingers. "So, five?"

He shook his head in wonderment and jotted a few anthropological field notes in the little notebook he always kept in his pocket. "And how many words went through *this*?" He tapped my head with a wicked smile.

"Enough to make me wish there was an off switch," which had always been true.

We were sun and moon, but it didn't matter on the night we met: 7:52 p.m. on April 5, 2013—the exact moment of sunset, though I didn't realize it when he texted me this exact meeting time, a pair of coordinates (30.2747° N, 97.9406° W), and a reference picture of a clay star crudely baked into a block of cement. *Meet me on the star,* he wrote. It was a plain-looking star with five terra-cotta tips revolving around a bright blue square with a crack down the middle. The plainness was deceptive. When I typed in the coordinates, they revealed the terra-cotta star inlaid right in front of the most ostentatious building in the entire Austin skyline—the Texas State Capitol.

At 7:20 p.m., I checked my lipstick, practiced what I hoped was a seductive smile, and walked out the front door of my one-room studio. The pink-granite dome of the Texas State Capitol was typically a thirty-minute walk, but that night I covered it in twenty. I moved in long, brisk strides down the sidewalk—an attempt to shake off nerves. I wasn't nervous about the usual things one might worry about when meeting an online suitor—that Jeff would turn out to be a balding C++ programmer, or secretly married with a dozen kids, or *really* into latex, or the proud owner of every Beanie Baby model since 1993. I was nervous because I had the impression that some interplanetary body was barreling towards the Capitol, preparing to sweep me into its orbit.

I reached the star before Jeff did. He didn't appear until dusk, when the streetlights along Congress Street flickered to life. I saw him then—a pair of canary yellow pants winding their way towards the front steps of the dome where I was waiting. He walked right up to the star and boldly kissed me on the cheek. That's where it started, in a small world that contained everything within itself: long canary pants, a terra-cotta star, the perfect arc of the dome, and above it all, the last streaks of the April sun.

. . .

We were inseparable after that night, though there was never any formal arrangement. Both of us agreed that, at this stage of the game, defining our romance was *passé* and unnecessary. It was all very modern.

He taught environmental science at the University of Texas at Brownsville, five hours to the south on the Mexican border, but he was applying for a new position in Austin and drove up or took the Greyhound whenever he could. On the weekends, we'd lie in my bed and compose far-fetched stories. We'd guess the ways our paths had crossed in other bodies and eras. Maybe he was the calico cat that once purred in my lap. Maybe he robbed my stagecoach on the road to Flagstaff. Maybe we warmed our hands at the same fire on a frigid night on the Mongolian steppe. Maybe one day we'd fly a starship across the universe divide, like that old Highwayman song.

OkCupid, the online dating site where we met, has a black-box algorithm that seemed to support our chemistry (at least in this lifetime). Our online profiles had been assigned a generous 99-percent compatibility rating (though for all I knew, the metric was generated in a cauldron of rose petals and blond locks of cherub hair). Sound or not, the number gave me an extra hit of confidence when, after just a month, we found ourselves sitting at my kitchen table in a state of morning undress, apprehensively eyeing my laptop screen. We were one click away from reserving two one-way tickets to Istanbul and a pair of return tickets from London.

The trip was his idea. He was already planning on travelling from Istanbul to London for his annual summer trip, but over the last week his "I'm going to Istanbul" had evolved into *"we're* going to Istanbul." That's how we ended up hunched over my table, daring ourselves to hit the purchase button.

"This could be a huge mistake," I said.

"Running off with some guy you just met online? What's the worst that could happen?" he said, slipping his hand around my waist like an old habit.

We laughed and hit the button.

At the time, it didn't seem unreasonably reckless to travel to the opposite side of the world after a month of dating—risky, maybe, but not reckless. Jeff was one of those rare figures who simply appeared and assumed his place, as if the bond had always been there and he was just confirming it with his corporeal form. We could skip the intros and get on with the adventure.

On the other hand, even if we had perished together on an eighteenth-century schooner, there were still practical details that had to be worked out. There were histories to exchange and timelines to establish: family trees, past lovers, old wounds, long-held quirks, the source of the jagged scar on his lower back, the origin of my crooked smile. We needed to catch up on our current incarnations.

One thing was guaranteed: the road would pry the stories out of us. Travel, with all of its glorious disorientation, shifting time zones, foreign skylines, and incomprehensible exchanges, had a way of wearing people down to their raw, messy (sometimes drunk, sometimes sick) under-layers. If Jeff had Parisian hospital escapades lurking in his past, I had my own trunk of secrets waiting to spill out in the open. Jaime should have also quizzed Jeff on how well he knew *me*. . . .

"I have a minor mental crisis on my record," I'd confessed in an early OkCupid correspondence with Jeff. It was a low-key mention, carefully dropped in a stream of brazen flirting. "Sounds interesting," he said. I hadn't been particularly forthcoming on the finer details—like how deeply I had tumbled down the rabbit hole after college graduation or how very recently I had climbed back out of it.

When we booked the tickets, I didn't mention that the trip to Istanbul was the first major flight I'd been stable enough to board in years. I said nothing about how radical it was just to leave the confines of my studio. He didn't know that I was still registering the reality of a recovery I never expected to reach, that the trip to Istanbul was an expression of a new, insatiable hunger for the world beyond my door.

Only a ravenous woman would agree to the sort of summer trip Jeff casually described in his third OkCupid email (long before he knew my last name or if I actually looked like the solemn, crooked-mouth girl in my profile picture). He didn't do luxury summer vacations. There were no resort packages or palm-thatched cabanas on white sandy beaches. He flew into one country and out of another with zero hotels, zero reservations, and zero itineraries between Airport A and Airport B. In my eyes, the fly-by-night style was adventure enough, but for Jeff it was just the beginning. He typically boarded the plane with nothing but a credit card, iPhone charger, and passport stuffed into his back pocket. What would happen after that was anyone's guess—that was the thrill.

Wandering the world with no baggage was one of the more radical pitches that popped into my OkCupid inbox (in the running with so many BDSM sex invitations and marriage proposals), but I didn't dismiss it right out of hand. I'd taken my post-recovery mantra from the poet Rilke's *Book of Hours*. "Let everything happen to you," he wrote. "Beauty and terror."

In the initial four weeks of definition-free dating, Jeff and I had accounted for beauty with weekend drives through the wildflower carpets of the Texas Hill Country and long, desultory walks down the back alleys of Austin. Terror was crossed off the list the day Jeff officially asked me to come along on his baggage-less jaunt. The proposal came without warning as we were crossing the Congress Street Bridge. I was studying the red and yellow kayaks scattered across Lady Bird Lake like candy sprinkles when he suddenly announced, "I wasn't joking about the trip. You should come with me."

I stopped breathing when he said the words. Jeff had been travelling since 1996, and of the seventy countries stamps in his passport, he'd stepped foot in sixty of them by himself, with no companions. He prized his freedom of movement like a Tea Party Republican prizes the constitutional right to bear arms. Leaving backpacks and suitcases behind was shocking, but it was even more shocking that he'd asked me to come along at all.

The intensity of his request reminded me of the scene in *Love In the Time of Cholera* when Florentino Ariza proposes to the love of his life, Fermina Daza. Fermina, wracked with uncertainty, goes to her Aunt Escolástica, who passionately advises her, "Tell him yes. Even if you are dying of fear, even if you are sorry later, because whatever you do, you will be sorry all the rest of your life if you say no."

I had plenty of reasons to say no. I hardly knew Jeff. My income constantly flirted with the poverty line. I was still tending to my fledgling sanity. And yet the words flew out of my mouth and into the warm lake air as if they had wings of their own, "Yes. I'm in." It was an instinctual, physical "yes"—a bone level, gut-guided judgment that preceded the speed of thought. I was getting on that plane. Even if I was sorry later.

. . .

Jeff reached back and put his hand on my knee as Jaime pulled into the drop-off lane in front of Terminal D.

"You ready?" he asked.

"It's not too late to change your mind," said Jaime, chiming in.

I put my hand on top of Jeff's, "Jaime, there's no turning back now."

"I know," he joked, "But you should really call me if Jeff makes a break for the Bastille."

"Don't listen to him," teased Jeff, "He's just trying to get your number."

The three of us climbed out and congregated in front of the car, where the differences between the two old friends were even more obvious. Jeff's travel uniform was composed of lobster-red chinos, a lightweight striped sweater, and his great-grandfather's gray Open Road Stetson, which he had opted to bring at the very last minute. Jaime looked formal in a navy tie and tailored office suit. (Jeff said he'd always been put together like that; he used to carry a briefcase to high school.) I could smell cologne as he leaned in to hug us good-bye. "Okay, for real. You guys take care of each other. I'll see you in three weeks."

And then he was gone and we were through the sliding doors and inside the crowded terminal. Morning passengers brushed past—paper coffee cups in one hand, rolling bags in the other. The only thing we all shared in common was the collective movement towards *somewhere else*—one of the far-away cities glowing with promise on the departure screens. We headed for the check-in desk, where a flight attendant waved us forward. She was polished, with a perfect chignon and a navy scarf neatly knotted around her neck.

"Any bags to check to Istanbul today?" she asked, as she scanned our passports.

"Trying to quit," Jeff told her, matter-of-factly. "No bags at all, actually."

She paused to look up from her computer. "I'm sorry. You don't have any bags to check or you don't have any bags, period?"

"We don't have any bags, period," he said, leaning into the laminate counter to disclose that juicy tidbit of gossip. "We're going just like this." Jeff pointed to me, Exhibit A: no suitcase at my feet, no zippered tote, no hiker's backpack with sleeping roll attached. Nothing but a small leather purse.

The flight attendant raised a dubious eyebrow at me—the one not wearing lobster-red pants—as if to say, "Is he serious?"

"Unfortunately, he's telling the truth," I said. "This is it for the next twenty-one days."

"Oh dear," she said, horrified, like I'd just announced I planned to take up topless pole dancing. "Are you sure?"

Hell, no. I'm not sure. When it came to this trip, I could count the things I was sure about on one hand: I was sure I was in seat 32A on a flight to Turkey and I was sure I was in way over my head.

Standing in an airport with no baggage is a lot like the dream where you show up to a party and discover you're the only one who forgot to get dressed. I felt naked. Unmoored. Weightless. *I have nothing. We have nothing.* My head was light with the nothingness. Without a suitcase to hold me down,

I felt dangerously at risk of floating up and away towards the skylights of Terminal D—like Mary Poppins, sans her magic satchel.

And what was a suitcase anyway? It was just an object—a container for other objects—bound together with zippers, fibre, and stitching. It was a simple carrying device and yet, without one, I was disoriented, caught off guard. There was an overwhelming impulse to stretch out my arms and fill the empty space with something, anything with weight and bulk. A goose feather pillow. A sack of red potatoes. A furry Maine coon cat. In my twenty-five years of existence I'd never been without at least a few things I could wrap my arms around and declare my own. To walk out the door empty-handed was utterly foreign.

In the days leading up to our departure, I'd attempted to compensate for the nothingness by assembling the perfect travel outfit—as if the right combination of odour-absorbent fabric, multipocketed cargo pants, and Teva sandals could ward off the perils of wearing the same clothes for twenty-one days straight. But like everything else in the story, I ended up with something completely unexpected: an exquisite, bottle-green, button-down, cotton dress with a band of delicate embroidery just above the knees. It was bright, flattering, well tailored, and completely impractical. Yet the impracticality was the very thing that made it so appealing. If I was going to wander the earth empty-handed, why not crank up the surreal-o-meter with an unexpected touch of elegance?

We spent our last night in the USA at Jaime's suburban house in Houston. Jeff insisted on setting the morning alarm at an ungodly hour so he could wake up and record a scientific log of every last item we were bringing. He was an obsessive documenter, constantly filming artifacts from his daily life—mundane conversations in the car, English muffins at breakfast, naps at the park. Regardless of the subject matter, he routinely deposited the clips onto a hard drive without so much as glancing at the contents.

The sun hadn't even risen when I found him in the kitchen, meticulously arranging the contents of my wallet on Jaime's wooden kitchen island, which had been converted into a vector grid. On the left, the total sum of his trip items were neatly folded and displayed at right angles to each other: one pair of cherry-red chinos, one Stetson cowboy hat, one pair of underwear, one pair of socks, a striped cotton shirt, an iPhone, a pair of earbuds, a charging cord, half a toothbrush, half a map of Eastern Europe, his notebook, a mechanical pencil, two hundred dollars in cash, one credit card, and his passport. All of it fit in his pockets.

On the right half were my things, folded and perfectly aligned: one green dress, three pairs of underwear, a cotton scarf, a black bra, a stick of lavender deodorant, a whole toothbrush, the retainer I'd been wearing since I was sixteen, a contact lenses case, a pair of backup glasses, two tampons, an iPhone, an iPad Mini, one notebook, one pen, my passport, a tiny black shoulder purse, a stack of cowboy magnets to hand out as Texas souvenirs, and a tube of cherry ChapStick.

"Morning, baby. It's time to get naked," said Jeff.

"I wish that were an invitation for naughty kitchen sex, but it's not, is it?" I said, pouring myself a cup of coffee.

It wasn't. The final step of the documentation process, Jeff informed me, was a timed packing exercise, in the nude, on camera. "What if Jaime walks in?" I protested. He was still asleep, Jeff assured me. We would do it fast. *Fine, fine.* I gave him the evil eye as I prepared to disrobe. The whole trip was an exercise in naked vulnerability. My bathrobe slipped to the ceramic kitchen tile as morning sunlight began to filter through the window over the sink. I was stark naked in Jaime's kitchen, my bare skin prickling under the air-conditioning vent. Jeff snapped on the camera with one hand and started the timer with the other. He waved at me to start.

It took me eight minutes to pack for a trip across the world. I stretched my arms through the emerald dress, inhaling the new cotton smell that would soon be masked by sweat and beer. Fully dressed, I carefully placed every item in my purse and slipped into a pair of thin leather sandals. And that was it. Eight minutes. I couldn't shake the feeling that I'd forgotten something.

"Not bad," said Jeff, clearly impressed.

His packing time was two minutes and thirty-one seconds—mostly because he threw on his clothes like his high school girlfriend's dad had just pulled into the driveway. When the kitchen island was clear, he raced out of the kitchen, down the hallway, and out Jaime's front door, whooping into the morning like one of the renegade Lost Boys. His pants were so bright that if he'd stretched out on the manicured lawn, Google Earth satellites would have picked up a small blazing red "V" just north of the Gulf of Mexico.

I briefly wondered if I'd still be fond of the blazing pants man by the time we checked into Heathrow for our return flight. Two people moving light and unencumbered through a series of unpredictable events sounded like a Zen haiku, but the combination of jet lag, customs lines, and crusty underwear was more akin to a ruthless speed date. Our compatibility (or lack thereof) would be rapidly evident. But in a way, the ending didn't matter: I was thrusting myself back to the world in a bottle-green dress.

Jeff came back to the porch and gave me a coffee-breath kiss. "Should we wake Jaime up?"

"Yep," I said, breathing in the humid morning air. "It's time to go."

CHAPTER 2 | Now We Wander

My sense of direction is subpar. The shortcoming has nothing to do with a lack of attention to my environment. It's more that my internal compass has always aligned with the poetic instead of the practical. In my neighbourhood, I know exactly where bees built a hive in a spiked Dasylirion bush and I can walk right to the spot where wild rosemary grows in fragrant scrubby clusters. I can't, however, give clear directions to the nearest gas station—mostly because I've never memorized the cardinal directions. I follow in the way of the naturalist John Muir, who wrote, "As long as I live, I'll hear waterfalls and birds and winds sing. I'll interpret the rocks, learn the language of flood, storm, and the avalanche."

Once, when Jeff and I were driving down I-35 from Austin to San Antonio, I pointed towards a cluster of glowing lights in the distance, "Doesn't downtown San Antonio look like a galaxy at night?"

"That's a cement plant, my dear," he smiled. "We're fifty miles north of San Antonio."

Still, romantic-era navigational methods aside, I can usually give a correct answer when asked to identify which continent I'm standing on. That wasn't the case when Jeff and I unstretched our cramped legs in the arrivals lobby of Atatürk Airport.

Istanbul is the only world city that straddles two continents. Crisscrossed by gargantuan bridges and a fleet of ferries, the Bosphorus Strait strikes right through the heart of the city, dividing east from west, Asia from Europe. During our initial flight descent, I'd been distracted by my mental poetry of the Mediterranean (*a wide, blue picnic blanket rippling in the sun*) and the fleets of gray shipping barges cutting through the water (*flocks of metal ducks*). Jeff was out cold on my shoulder, mouth slightly parted, glasses askew. He didn't flinch when the pilot's voice crackled onto the intercom. "Sunny, clear afternoon, ladies and gentlemen. Beautiful day in Istanbul. Eighty degrees on the ground. Light breeze from the northeast. Sit back and relax, we'll be landing shortly."

The wheels groaned out of the belly of the plane as we began the descent. I could see palm trees and minarets launching upwards like slender needles stuck in the earth. "If one had but a single glance to give the world, one should gaze on Istanbul," said Alphonse de Lamartine, a nineteenth-century French writer. Unlike Lamartine's, my first gaze on Istanbul was unequivocally modern: the teeming arrivals terminal—visa signs swirling with the flourishes of the Turkish alphabet; doors to quiet *masjid* prayer rooms where travelers kneeled facing east; screens with connecting flights to Beirut, Dubai, and Cairo; and designer headscarves in the customs line.

In the rush of arrival, I somehow failed to register whether the airport was on the European side or the Asian one. It briefly occurred to me that I had no idea which continent I was on as I battled my flight-rumpled hair in the bathroom (though at that moment, I was more occupied with the ragged reflection in the mirror than my exact geographical position). Jeff and I would have to skip the early, always-look-attractive stage of dating. I was already beginning to resemble the whiffling Jabberwock of Lewis Carroll fame. The roots of my hair were dark-tinged with grease. My eyes were dim crescents. My dress smelled like stale fingers on airplane cushions. My armpits had begun their gradual descent into bacterial petri dishes. *Oh well.* I slathered on a fresh layer of deodorant, swept my hair up into a greasy bun, and headed back out to the arrivals lobby.

Jeff was leaning against a column busily adding his flight stub to a notebook full of other random ephemera—business cards, sand, feathers, toothpicks, dog hair. I yawned as he snapped the book shut. "So what now?"

Beneath the Stetson his eyes were glittering with excitement, like he'd downed a shot of espresso while I was in the bathroom. "I vote we hop on a train toward town and get off at a random stop." He announced his plan as if it were the obvious next step.

"Really?" I said slowly, "You don't think we should get oriented first?"

He just shrugged nonchalantly. "I'm sure we'll figure it out along the way."

The etymology of the word "travel" can be traced back to the word "travail," which brings to mind the sorts of arduous journeys that blister your ankles, burn your calves, and provide a mélange of reasons to wish you had never left home at all. The reality is that every good and wonderful thing tends to be accompanied by some degree of travail. For every stunning overlook and iconic selfie there are bound to be long lines, wailing babies on planes, or abysmally low blood sugar.

I had gone nearly twenty-four hours without entering an REM state. Unlike Jeff, I'd spent most of the transatlantic flight attempting to fold my body in an origami shape that didn't cut off blood flow to critical limbs (a mission that earned me nothing but a shallow nap and a stiff neck). My initial gaze upon Istanbul wasn't breathtaking: it was exhausted and full of crusty eye rheum.

Travail also seemed inevitable in the lodging department. If we stuck to our self-imposed experimental guidelines (and vagabond budget), hotels were off-limits and hostels were a last resort. Our plan was to stay with locals via Couchsurfing.com—a global community where locals host travellers in their homes for free as a form of cultural exchange. But despite sending a dozen couch requests to hosts in Istanbul, we'd accumulated zero invitations, which seemed to imply that we might be roaming the streets of Istanbul, gathering strips of cardboard for makeshift beds in the park.

The thought of leaving my bed up to the capriciousness of chance provoked a surprising inner panic. Soap and pillows weren't going to drop out of the sky at a random train stop. Instead of freewheeling through the city, I felt we needed to hold a Camp David strategy session. We needed a map. We needed an Internet connection to send out a volley of emergency Couchsurfing requests. We needed to establish which continent we were on.

Out of habit, I calculated a mental list of The Very Worst That Could Happen. There was a chance that we'd end up lost, exhausted, and temporarily roofless, but were we courting imminent disaster by jumping on a random train? *Not really.* One night on a bench probably wouldn't do me in. Jeff certainly didn't seem to think so. He was still leaning against the column, lazily smiling at me, a queue of taxis in the background. He appeared to be supremely unconcerned by the possibility of cardboard beds. In fact, in the few weeks since we'd been together I couldn't remember him worrying about anything except whether or not I had peanut butter chunk ice cream in the freezer. He was confident about his ability to cook something up with whatever ingredients were on hand in the moment—the very exercise we'd come all this way to practice together.

I sighed and ran the back of my hand against his cheek, already splinter sharp with a day's worth of stubble. "Okay, cowboy. Where's the train?" If the drifter strategy failed to work I'd insist on a more orthodox approach to room and board, but—for tonight at least—I'd take a chance on the unknown.

. . .

I knew a thing or two about being lost. I'd earned a first-rate education when I wandered off into the wild territories of my own mind for two harrowing years. Jeff didn't know it at the time, but when he met me on the Capitol steps it had only been four months since I'd found my way back.

I'm still not sure why I lost my way in the first place. Maybe it was sheer neuroticism. Maybe it was my oversensitivity to the human condition or the disillusionment of the 2008 economic meltdown, a consequence of avarice and greed. Maybe it was a deep-seated longing for the certainty of my evangelical Christian childhood, where every last biblical jot and tittle was whispered from God's mouth to disciple's ear. Or maybe it was dread over my realization that Jesus wasn't some friendly fellow in the sky doling out purpose—that the task of crafting something meaningful out of my blip of a life rested squarely on my own shoulders.

Maybe I simply needed to get lost in the same way that forests need wildfires to burn away old undergrowth. All

I know is that in the fall of 2010 I was composing lofty statements of purpose for graduate school, and by the time the daffodils bloomed in 2011, I was curled around a toilet every day, dry-heaving with panic.

The lost-ness went by different names. My parents called it a "difficult phase." My grandfather said I was knocking my mid-life crisis out a few decades early (always ahead of the curve!). My doctor said I'd come down with a severe "mental disorder" brought on by a chemical imbalance inside my brain. He prescribed a silver packet of tranquilizers. My therapist said I'd embarked on a dark night of the soul and advised me to hold on tight because the only way out was *through*. The long-dead French philosophers confirmed I was suffering a classic existential crisis—a formal way of saying I'd run out of decent reasons to get out of bed in the morning.

Whatever the label, I hoped the paralysing anxiety settling into my gut was a temporary thing, like a Jack Daniel's hangover that would fade after a good night's sleep and a greasy cheeseburger. I was anxious to get back to normal— to grad school programs and blooming literary ambitions. I hunted for the familiar in the same way a lost hiker hunts for a recognisable bend in the river or an unusual outcropping of rock. But normal had vanished, a trail gone cold. My inner landscape turned foreign.

Unbeknownst to me, one of the hallmarks of severe anxiety is the overwhelming sense that one has been severed from the reality that everyone else inhabits. I felt like I'd floated out of my body and up to the ceiling, where I observed "normal" people going about their daily business from a great remove. My world was collapsing into a dark pinhole. Places that had formerly seemed harmless were suddenly threatening: the house I shared with my roommate, the route I drove to work, Mexican restaurants, the Target parking lot. Anxiety was a lens that reduced every aspect of my life to a series of deadly, worst-case scenarios.

The only time I felt safe was for the first ten seconds of each morning. For that short window, I briefly forgot about the fear. But, then, as I opened my eyes, it would come rushing back: a heavy weight on my chest, shallow breaths, racing adrenaline, waves of nausea, and erratic thoughts like an infinite snarl of yarn. By noon, I often felt like I'd just raced a 10K marathon.

My attempts to rein in my dive-bombing mental health manifested as an unusual eating disorder (despite the fact that

I loved to cook and had never owned a bathroom scale). One afternoon I simply couldn't eat anymore. My appetite vanished, my saliva dried up like a Texas creek in July, and food often came back up as soon as I swallowed. Doctors were at a total loss for a diagnosis. I just assumed something was fundamentally cracked in my brain. It never occurred to me that anyone with constant, pulse-racing anxiety would struggle to digest food or that it wasn't uncommon for eating disorders to accompany nervous breakdowns. ("I could usually induce her to eat a certain amount," wrote Leonard of his wife, Virginia Woolf, during a period of madness, "but it was a terrible process.")

When my ribcage started to show in the summer of 2011 it was obvious I could no longer keep up any outward pretense of normal. It was time to admit it. In quick succession, I resigned from my management job at a jewelry studio, informed my roommate that I was moving out of the house we jointly leased, and rolled a suitcase back into my teenage bedroom. It was either my parents' house in the Fort Worth suburbs or a trip to the psych ward.

"Looks like my life's over at the ripe age of twenty-three," I told my mom. It was an early summer morning. Usually I'd be tan from swimming, but instead, I was lying in bed, gaunt and failing to land a joke. My mother, Sarah, sat across from me in a black IKEA rocking chair. I was lucky that in addition to being my parent, she was also one of my closest friends. Tall and intense with short strawberry-blonde hair, she'd weathered a few mental storms of her own. Her life hadn't exactly followed a traditional track either.

She jumped on a Greyhound out of San Francisco two months after graduating high school. From there, she drifted through the late 1970s. In Seattle, she lived with two Vietnam vets who medicated their undiagnosed PTSD with cards and drink. When that fell through she moved into a communist co-op committed to dismantling capitalism and the patriarchy. She performed folk songs in Pike's Place Market, operated a tractor on an Idaho grain farm, waitressed in Vermont, and bussed back and forth across the country with nothing but a bag and a guitar. At the age of twenty-two, when she became pregnant with my older sister Anna after a short-lived relationship, she too moved back in with her mother in Venice Beach.

She eyed me calmly from the rocking chair. "How do you know what your life will be like? Are you a fortune-teller?"

"I don't need to be," I said dramatically. "It's obvious.

Everyone I know is either going off to graduate school or internships and my top goal for today is to get out of bed and eat a peanut-butter-jelly sandwich without puking it back up. That doesn't exactly scream 'bright future.'"

She paused, measuring her words, and then said, "I wonder what would happen if you quit trying to be normal and just let yourself be exactly where you are?"

"What, just let all this happen?"

"You might be surprised," she laughed. "Maybe life as you know it has shifted. But just because you're lost doesn't mean you can't explore."

. . .

Jeff jerked a thumb out the train window, "Let's try this stop." We stumbled out into a broad Istanbul thoroughfare. The dusty street was a cacophonous symphony of taxi horns, sirens, and clanging trams. It looked central, but I had no idea. On either side of the street, six-story buildings were lined shoulder to shoulder. Red flags, air-conditioning units, satellite dishes, and mini shade awnings spilled out of windows that overlooked a crowded sidewalk lined with palms. I shaded my eyes and peered down the street in either direction.

"So, now we wander?" I said.

"Yep. Now we wander," said Jeff.

"Right or left?" Not that it mattered.

"Left," said Jeff, hooking down the boulevard, his Stetson bobbing through a swarm of pretzel vendors and sun-visored tourists—almost like he actually knew where he was going. For him, movement was an art. Back in Austin he once recounted how, in college, his father had paid for him to take a career aptitude test. After days of measuring analytical prowess, hand-eye coordination, and pattern recognition, the results declared him a promising candidate—not for business consultant or entrepreneur—but for riverboat captain. Somehow, it fit. I could easily imagine him guiding a steamboat down the Mississippi, intuitively maneuvering the fickle moods of the river with a soggy, unlit cigar clenched between his teeth, some kind of Mark Twain rascal.

I was more than happy for Jeff to play the role of guide. The two of us had already established our roles in rambling walks across Austin. I processed the magic of the environment. He moved us through it. I was poet. He was steersman. It wasn't that I was totally incapable of navigation (I could get by if I focused hard) but that handing off the compass allowed me to orient to a completely different set of markers. Like light. In Texas, where it's mostly broad and flat, the sun presses into your shoulders and the clouds congregate in cumulus mountains that cast shadows across the dirt for miles. But in Istanbul, the summer light is ethereal. It glitters gold in the afternoon, refracted into the air on all sides by the Black Sea, the Sea of Marmara, and the Bosphorus.

As poet and steersman, we were following a long tradition of indiscriminate wandering. Taking the pulse of an urban landscape on foot was hardly a new idea. The French had their own word for urban ramblers: the *flâneur*. The nineteenth-century *flâneur* was a modern, exploratory stroller who took in the boulevards and arcades as a "moving photograph of urban experience," as the French journalist Victor Fournel put it. The poet Charles Baudelaire also captured the process with lyrical flair: "For the perfect flâneur, for the passionate spectator, it is an immense joy to set up house in the heart of the multitude, amid the ebb and flow of movement, in the midst of the fugitive and the infinite. To be away from home and yet to feel oneself everywhere at home; to see the world, to be at the centre of the world, and yet to remain hidden from the world."

To observe the streets of Istanbul through the eyes of an urban *flâneur* was to notice that I wasn't the only one unsure of which continent I was standing on. The city of seven hills has continuously shifted with the swell and decay of empires and was, even now, negotiating its identity within a complex juxtaposition of East and West, religious and secular, modern and traditional. On the sidewalk, Turkish women in fluorescent miniskirts and silver hoop earrings brushed past other women in full hijab. Political posters for pro-secular supporters hung on walls that echoed with the *ezan* calls to prayer (nearly the only Arabic one could hear in the city). Sleek, modern façades with small cafés and boutique hotels were buttressed up against old stone walls that looked as if they've been sitting since the days when the city went by Constantinople.

Evidence of the Ottoman Empire was ubiquitous in the pointed minarets that punctured the sky, and the steamy Ottoman bathhouses, and the domes upon domes in the distance, stacked like upturned teacups. But the city also held reminders that Istanbul was once the centre of the Byzantine Empire—a city where Orthodox Christians prayed to Jesus, Son of God, for over a thousand years. The remnants were still visible in the outline of the hippodrome track where the Emperor Constantine watched high-stakes chariot races, and in the vaulted cupola of the Hagia Sophia, the largest cathedral in the world for nearly a millennium.

Neither Jeff nor I spoke as we drifted in and out of noisy streets. It was a comfortable silence. We moved at whim, our route governed by intrigue: a man in a dark cap shaving a slice of lamb off a vertical *kebab* rotisserie, an aproned woman tending a display of mountains of Turkish delight cut into perfect sticky-powdered squares, or a sweaty, bargaining trinket salesman. We were caught up in a sensory parade, a blur of dense throngs, street hawkers, flags, seagulls, and the afternoon *İkindi* call to prayer (when shadows cast by objects are equal to their heights).

After some length of time, I signaled Jeff to cut off into a cobbled side alley away from the din of the main street. It was immediately quiet except for a few shopkeepers sorting through shoeboxes and an ancient man sitting on the corner squeezing orange juice from a metal press that looked like a relic from the sixteenth century. I traded a lira and a mangled Turkish "thank you" for a small cup. *Teşikkür ederim.* We sipped the juice on a shaded staircase nearby. Warm and frothy sweet. The steps smelled like stale piss, but it was cool and still. Paradise.

I closed my eyes and sunk my head into Jeff's shoulder. It was late afternoon and we still had no place to stay. I still didn't know which continent I was on. Our *flâneur* roam hadn't cured me of the desire for psychological handrails. I was still disturbed by the vast openness of the moment, though there was another part of me—a wild, and curious part—that was beginning to wonder if there wasn't something sacred about intentionally wandering with nothing.

"It's a rare thing to be lost, isn't it?" I said. "I mean, you catch a news clip every once in a while about a hiker who disappears in the woods or a Cessna pilot who turns up in a snowdrift, but for the most part, you know exactly where you stand on the planet—down to a precise red dot on a Google map. Walking around without a GPS lady who tells you to turn right at the fork is sort of old-fashioned, right? Like, it's obsolete to be unaware of where you are in space."

"That's what's interesting," said Jeff, with his eyes closed. "When you're lost you can't go from Point A to Point B, because you don't know your relation to either point in the first place. When there's no Point A, Point B ceases to exist." He was always reciting these little made-up proverbs. It was impossible to say whether they were nuggets of profound Yoda wisdom or complete bullshit delivered with a straight face. He probably didn't know the difference himself.

"Okay." I rolled my eyes. "But the *idea* of having no Point B is alarming. Like, even though I know I'm not in any mortal danger, I feel alarmed, because I can't predict where we're going to sleep tonight or when I'm going to be able to wash the grease out of my hair. We're just floating along, and I have to assume that I'll be able to handle whatever pops out of the ether."

"Well, I popped out of the OkCupid ether, right?" said Jeff. "And maybe we don't need to 'handle' anything. Just hop on the A train, kick back with a gin in the drink car, and watch what happens."

· · ·

Jeff was constantly daring the universe to show him something new. "Everything's more or less the same," he would say. "So why not have some fun?" His version of "fun" usually involved toeing the line of one or more widely accepted social norms—a trait that was equal parts attractive and frightening.

On our first date, he confessed that in the wake of his

divorce he'd been illegally living in his university office for the last eight months. We were sitting at a shadowy, wax-covered table in an underground bar right across from the Capitol. The Cloak Room was more of a den than a bar. There weren't more than five small tables, though the room seemed bigger in the reflection of a long mirror snaking around the back wall. I could hardly make out my hand in front of my face as I carefully descended the long basement staircase. The only light came from a glowing jukebox in the corner and a strand of Christmas lights wrapped around the bar counter. It was dripping with Texas noir.

"Let's just say some sketchy shit has gone down in this bar," Jeff said as we sat down. "Congressmen, hookers, under-the-table deals. People still smoke in here even though smoking's been banned for ten years. The rule is: smoke if you want to, but if the sheriff's department busts the place, you pay the five-thousand-dollar tab."

The way he said it I could almost smell cigar smoke and cheap perfume. Or maybe it was the hairspray the blonde bartender was using to coax her '50s bouffant into place. "That's Bev," said Jeff. "She's been here since Nixon. Moody as hell, but she's sweet if you give her a little love and some Elvis on the jukebox." Jeff winked and went to the bar to order two glasses of tequila. *Good evening, young lady. Herradura Silver. Neat.*

We clinked glasses.

"So, you're telling me that *no one* has caught on to your squatter setup at school?" I said.

"Nope. It's foolproof," he assured me. "I hide my sleeping bag in the recycling bin and keep my clothes in two lockers at the gym. No one asks any questions. Plus, I've got this giant painting of my great-great-grandfather Abner on the wall. He's this baby in a little lace dress. Super creepy. Abner cut his own throat with a pocketknife, so I tell everyone my office is haunted."

I raised an eyebrow. "So, you have a suicidal baby on the wall and you keep your bed in a recycling bin."

He looked briefly repentant. "Look, I don't usually come out with all this on the first date, but I was married for six years. Then I got divorced. There was never anything particularly wrong. Just a gradual cooling off. We were sleeping in separate bedrooms. I didn't want that to be an example of marriage for my daughter, Sibel."

He took a sip of tequila, a brief *fermata* to gauge my reaction to the divulgement of daughter and ex-wife. "Fair enough," I said, unbothered by the revelation.

"After the separation I needed to shake up my life a little," he continued, "You know, classic mid-life crisis. Do something crazy. I had a garage sale, sold everything I owned for a dollar apiece, and moved into my office. Turns out I needed to downsize for the dumpster anyway."

I tucked my hair behind my ear and leaned closer into him. "I'm sorry. The dumpster?"

He pulled out his notebook and feverishly sketched out a six-by-six box. "Would you consider dating a guy who lives in a trash can?"

Maybe? The dumpster was his latest social experiment, he informed me. It was a harebrained educational project he had somehow managed to talk the University of Brownsville president into sanctioning. Over the course of a year, he and a team of students, scientists, and engineers planned to transform a used 36-square-foot dumpster into a state-of-the-art tiny home. He would live in it during each renovation phase.

If it were someone else, I would have been shocked, but for some reason Jeff's dumpster scheme didn't surprise me. He knew how to play with reality the same way he knew how to play with my hands in the dark bar—the same way he knew to lean in, hold my face, and kiss me hard on the lips.

It was a long, hedonic first kiss—exactly the sort of sensuous act I'd resolved to avoid on the first date. I had nothing against casual encounters, but this was my first online date and I wanted to proceed with caution. To bolster my resolve I'd intentionally refrained from shaving my legs and earlier, in the bathroom, I'd stared into the mirror and whispered, "thou shalt not sleep with him until you know him better."

Hairy legs or no, the chances of sticking to my commandment seemed to fade with each passing minute. We had sparkling chemistry. He wasn't wearing cologne, but he smelled *right*. Musky sweet. I wanted to bury myself into his neck and inhale. But there would be no inhaling on Bev's watch. She went into an apoplectic fit over the second steamy first kiss.

"Oh, no. We don't do that here," she growled with a smoker's rasp. "Out!"

"Sorry, Bev," said Jeff. He grabbed my hand, gave Bev an impenitent wink goodbye, and then whisked me up the staircase faster than my resolve could fly.

. . .

"Should we move on?" asked Jeff, gently shaking me awake. A Turkish pop song was floating out of a distant window and I could smell hints of onion and olive oil in the air. The roofline had sliced the sun in half. I stood up and sleepily looked around. There was an Internet café a few cobbled blocks down. "You want to check email?" I asked. We had smartphones but they only worked with WiFi. Jeff nodded and we walked down to a small, stuffy room lined with twenty computers and a lone fan blowing in front of a young clerk who pointed us to two adjoining computers. I was lost even on the keyboard, which was similar to English, but just different enough that the letters in my email address sprouted dots and swirls.

"Hey, did you find the 'shift' key?" I asked Jeff. He didn't answer and when I looked over he was staring at his screen with a funny grin on his face.

"Guess what?" he said. "I just got an email from my friend Mohammad—this Iranian bicyclist I Couchsurfed with in Kazakhstan a few years ago. Turns out he's also in Istanbul for a few days and he's house sitting for this lady who—of course—is originally from Austin. He saw that we're in town and was wondering if we needed a place to stay. There's a queen air mattress in her living room."

I was incredulous. "So, what, that's it? We have a bed?"

"Yep," said Jeff triumphantly. "All we have to do is catch a five o'clock ferry over to the Asian side."

The Asian side. If we were heading to the Asian side, that meant we'd been wandering around the European continent for the last four hours. I leaned back against the rolling office chair, amazed that things had fallen into place with so little effort. I had no idea whether Mohammad's offer was a random, lucky fluke or if there truly was some invisible cord guiding us toward soap and pillows. All I knew was that, for tonight at least, I had a sink, a bed, and a warm body to share it with.

And that was enough.

CHAPTER 3 | Sunbeams and Snapping Jaws

The Asian side of Istanbul is homier and more working-class than the European side. At the Kadiköy ferry port, white-capped surge licked up the sides of old stone bulwarks where rows of fishermen stood hunched over poles. Mussel sellers hawked round trays glistening with rice-filled shells and lemon wedges. The air was salty and the sun was low. Mohammad was waiting for us a little ways down the Kadiköy boardwalk. Jeff spotted him as we worked our way down the ferry ramp in a swarming rush of evening commuters eager to get home.

Mohammad was a short, muscular man with dark curls, sport sunglasses, and a tight, tangerine cycling jersey. A bike leaned against his side. "You're going to love this guy," Jeff told me on the windy ferry ride over. "When I first met

Mohammad he had just biked from Iran to Kazakhstan—by way of Singapore."

Jeff bellowed down the boardwalk, "My brother, Axis of Evil!" Since first meeting Mohammad in Almaty, Kazakhstan, two years earlier, Jeff had taken great comedic pleasure in mocking the histrionic political relations between Iran and the United States. He gleefully referred to himself as the "Great Satan" (a creative title bestowed upon the United States in a 1979 speech by the Ayatollah Khomeini) and affectionately referred to Muhammad as the "Axis of Evil" (an homage to the similarly melodramatic title President George W. Bush assigned to Mohammad's home country of Iran during his 2002 State of the Union speech).

"My brother, I pray your plutonium supply is strong," he said, enfolding Mohammad in a hug.

Mohammad teased back, "I had a dream last night about your American freedom and democracy: my dream was empty."

Jeff giggled like a schoolgirl as he turned to introduce me. "Mohammad, I'd like you to meet Clara, my . . . uh . . . travel companion." There was an awkward, stumbling pause—a clear tell that we had chosen to bypass the *so-what-are-we?* conversation.

If we had mentioned labels in passing, it was only to half-jokingly point out that we were at a loss over which ones to use. "Travel companion" sounded like a formal phrase Queen Victoria might have intoned over high tea; "girlfriend" was far too soon (not to mention a minefield of commitment), and "friend" seemed to belie the fact that we typically shared a bed without wearing clothes. We were approaching the vagaries of modern romance with caution, refusing to label our bond unless it showed signs of longer-term promise. The occasional awkward pause was the price we paid.

But if there was awkwardness, Mohammad didn't seem to notice. He warmly shook my hand and removed his sunglasses, revealing a quiet pair of eyes that seemed older than his thirtysomething years. He struck me as one of those rare, earnest beings incapable of ulterior motives. His entire person radiated calm—not a surface calm, but the deep unshakable kind, earned through adversity.

"Mohammad is probably the closest I've ever come to meeting a real-life saint," Jeff informed me beforehand. "He spontaneously bikes around the world giving peace talks and planting trees with schoolchildren—all with zero plans and zero fundraising. I mean, come on, it's impossible to get more saintly than that."

Mohammad pointed a tanned arm towards the Kadiköy neighbourhood along the water. "I'm on the way to meet friends at a café. Would you like to join?" Jeff and I were both shaky with exhaustion, but it would have been rude to refuse after his generous invitation to host us. We followed him into Kadiköy, where the cobbled streets were stitched together in spider like grids. Narrow, shop-lined corridors fed into round, open-air plazas crisscrossed with fluttering crimson pennants. The Turkish flag—blood red with white star and waning crescent—hovered brightly over our heads from balconies and windows. In one plaza, a crowd clapped along to a band of bohemian folk musicians performing with stretched leather drums and an ornately stitched bagpipe. The swirl of red, the omnipresent Kemal Atatürk posters (revered father of secular Turkey), and the rhythmic *pound-pound-pound* of the drums reminded us that the entire country had recently been engulfed in waves of street protests against the autocratic style of the Turkish prime minister.

We could still faintly hear the drums when Mohammad stopped in front of a small outdoor café crowded with traditional low square tables, a cluster of tiny woven stools, and half a dozen cross-country Iranian bicyclists in full green and red regalia. "The U.S. embassy is *so* not going to be pleased," Jeff joked. There was a flurry of hugs and friendly hand-shakes amidst bike wheels, helmets, and Iranian cycling jerseys and then we lowered ourselves onto the stools for a round of black *çay* tea (pronounced "chai"), served in small tulip-shaped glasses on red-striped saucers.

Conversation was friendly if not limited. All we could collectively manage were basic English sentences supple-mented by hand gestures and rudimentary jokes. *Where am I from? I'm from Texas. Yes, George Bush is my neighbor. Yes, we ride horses to work. Except on Sundays when we pray to Jesus, watch football, and fire up the barbecue.*

Jeff dozed off against the wall after the first round of tea. Basic sentences had been exhausted and the Iranians had moved on to conversations that didn't require sign lan-guage. I took the opportunity to lean towards Mohammad. "Jeff told me a little about your story, but I'm curious to hear more. Planting trees on a bike isn't something that just hap-pens to someone."

Mohammad smiled, took a sip of *çay*, and settled his hands in his lap. "I'll tell you," he said. "It begins with a mountain."

It seems that ten years earlier he'd traveled with a

team of mountaineers to the base of a small mountain in northeastern Iran. They were training for an expedition up the Pamir Mountains, a difficult range in Central Asia. It was Ramadan and the walnut trees had just begun to turn gold. After dusk, when the fast was broken, the team began a moonlit trail run up the mountain. "At first it was like any other climb," he said, "but after a quarter mile, I was suddenly unable to move."

"What happened?" I said, stirring a sugar cube into my second cup.

"I was paralysed," Mohammad replied nonchalantly, as if full-body paralysis was on par with an empty stomach or a light headache. "I couldn't run. I couldn't move. It felt like a great surge of energy had glued my feet to the ground. The coach was angry. The team had to continue up the mountain without me."

Mohammad described the way he sat alone on the silent mountain, watching the lights flickering down in the valley, overwhelmed with the sense that something big was shifting out in the darkness. At some point, he called out to his mother. *Mum, everything is about to change.*

"Have you ever experienced this feeling?" Mohammad directed the question at me, his eyes suddenly ablaze. "The feeling that everything you know is about to be gone and you're a blind man, unable to see what will take its place?" He made a blunt sweeping motion with his hand. *Gone.*

"Oh, yeah," I said, locking eyes. "I'm well acquainted with that one."

"I didn't understand it," said Mohammad. "Everything was good."

He had just opened a business with his friend in his hometown. It was going well. He was making money. But after that night on the mountain, an old childhood dream of cycling around the world resurfaced with new urgency. He wanted to feel tires against pavement and plant a trail of trees along his route. It wasn't a practical life plan, but after a year of bicycle training and English lessons, the call of the road began to outweigh the stability of staying put.

"I was floating in a lake one day, asking the earth to give me a sign," said Mohammad. "And I felt the sun and sea laughing at me like a mother laughs at a child who's afraid of something new and strange. The laugh meant: *don't worry; nothing is wrong. I am right here with you.* So, I did it. I left my company and sold everything to prepare for my journey."

"And then what happened?"

Mohammad raised an eyebrow. "Everything fell apart!

No travel sponsors. No money. My girlfriend left. I had a broken hand and a shoulder injury. I almost lost hope."

"Sometimes that's the beginning," I said.

"Yes, exactly," said Mohammad, leaning back on his stool. "Falling apart is what led me to make the *real* leap: to begin my journey without any money—without knowing how I would sustain myself. I let go and decided I didn't need to do anything except listen and follow. It was up to the universe to provide the rest."

"Were you afraid?" I said, feeling a familiar thrill welling up in my chest.

"Of course!" he laughed. "I was terrified. But I've been on the road for ten years now. I've planted 957 trees in forty countries. Everything has been provided." Mohammad smiled like he knew a secret. "Life is about trust. Nothing happens until you take a step out. The universe gives nothing to those who do not trust."

. . .

The first thing I registered in the early glimmer of morning was a row of laundry drying on a windowsill beside a red Turkish flag. Striped socks, two pairs of underwear, and a green dress. I hardly remembered hanging the clothes to dry the night before, though I vaguely recalled running the armpits of my dress under soapy water in the bathroom sink and thinking: *this isn't so bad.* Exhaustion and jet lag had blurred the rest. I couldn't remember the sky going dark, or the bus ride to the flat, or the two flights of stairs, or the collapse into the squeaky plastic comfort of an air mattress in a stranger's window-lined living room. I couldn't remember where I'd found the fluorescent orange sheet now wrapped loose and toga-like around my naked torso.

In light of Mohammad's tale, the makeshift toga and the little row of laundry suddenly seemed underwhelming. Jeff and I were cruising around without baggage or plans for a meager three weeks while Mohammad had dedicated his entire existence to an affair with uncertainty. The sum of his possessions was loaded on the back of his bike. He had less than fifty dollars to his name at any given time. There was no house of comforts waiting back home, no credit card for the lean times.

We were just middle-class white Americans intentionally choosing to test the unknown. Large swathes of the global population have no assets, no possessions, and no certainty, a condition thrust upon them not as a deliberate choice, but as a lifelong fact of existence. And the halls of history are lined with illustrious figures who maintained a voluntary ultra-minimal lifestyle for a lot longer than three weeks. It was practically de rigueur for sages to do without. Gandhi breathed his last with less than ten possessions to his name, including his spectacles and sandals. Buddha renounced all worldly trappings when he left his palace to join the suffering of the world. The prophet Muhammad is said to have lived in a simple clay house with a cot and a pillow stuffed with palm leaves.

And then there's Jesus, the savior my parents raised me to revere. He was notorious for asking complete strangers to leave everything they owned and follow him. "Do not worry about your life," he admonished his disciples, "what you will eat; nor about the body, what you will put on. Life is more than food, and the body is more than clothing." Jesus was exactly the kind of character who would have had zero qualms about cruising out of Atatürk Airport with nothing but his robe and a loaf-and-fish sandwich.

The air mattress made a rustling plastic sound as Jeff began to stir beside me. I was always struck by how alien he looked without his thick-rimmed glasses. *It's like waking up with a stranger*, I would tell him. He would tease me back: *what do you know about waking up with strangers?*

"What are you thinking about?" he said, rolling over to squint at me.

"Nothing," I lied.

"Bullshit," he said. "The *wheeeeeeeels* are turning."

His body sank into a plastic valley as I rolled off the air mattress and pulled my black polka-dot underwear down from the window. They were cool from the morning air. The cotton was still slightly damp. I slipped them on anyway.

"I don't know," I said. "At the airport, the whole 'no bags' thing felt like such a risky, daredevil act. Everyone back home acted like we were attempting a lunar landing. *That's all you're bringing? Oh my god. Be safe.* And now—I don't know—I'm wondering if it's going to be sort of anticlimactic. You just run the clothes under some soap and water and hang them to dry—which, sure, is a little inconvenient, but nothing radical, like climbing Kilimanjaro or spearfishing for dinner. It's *laundry*. As far as the minimalist bit goes, we're basically Americans doing laundry abroad."

"Humans have been doing laundry since the loincloth," said Jeff, riffing off my train of thought. "Maybe it's the anticlimax that's radical. Not the cruising around sans bags."

"Could be," I said. "Newsflash! The world doesn't fall off its axis if you don't have a walk-in closet crammed with stuff!"

Jeff fished around for his glasses on the floor. "Hey, the trip just started. There's still plenty of time for the world to fall off its axis." He held up his hands as I tossed him his underwear. "You wanna get dressed and see the Hagia Sophia?"

. . .

We foraged for coffee in the wood-panelled kitchen, left a note for the still-sleeping Mohammad, and then retraced our steps back across the city: a crowded street bus, a hair-whipping ferry ride across the Bosphorus, and a short walk through the winding Old Town streets of Sultanahmet. It was easy to find our way. The Hagia Sophia is visible for miles with its elegant cascade of lofty buttresses, vaulted domes, half domes, and minarets, like the folds of an empress's gown. If buildings could grow roots, then the *Ayasofya* would have deep ones, stretching from the dusky coral façades, down through the old stone floors, and down even deeper to the soil itself—the same plot the foundation had rested on since

537 A.D. For over a thousand years, the Hagia Sophia—*Holy Wisdom*—was the largest church in all of Christendom and the seat of the Eastern Orthodox Church. The Ottomans, too, had recognised her rare beauty when they'd taken the city in 1453. Relics came down, minarets went up, and cathedral became mosque.

Now, as a museum, the basilica attracts millions of travelers, pilgrims, and devotees—a ripe opportunity for the tour hawkers and guidebook peddlers clustered around the entrance, hoping to capitalize on awe. As tourists approached, they lobbed calculated greetings. *Guten tag! Hallo! Privet! Parlez-vous français?* A short, keen-eyed salesman intercepted us in the ticket line: "Excuse me, where are you from?"

"No English," said Jeff. He regarded all salesmen as fellow members of his tribe—jokers, coyotes, and court jesters whose bells and whistles disguised a strategic eye. As such, they were fair game for subterfuge.

"Deutsch?" tried the salesman.

"*Nein,*" said Jeff solemnly.

"Français?"

"*Non.*"

"Russki?"

"*Nyet.*"

"Where are you *from*, my friend?" The salesman eyed Jeff's cowboy hat suspiciously.

Jeff knitted his brows and then, in a thick accent, announced, "*Transnistria.*" At this, the salesman gave up and set his sights on a Korean couple in matching polos, leaving us to pass through the imposing Imperial Door in peace.

It was immediately obvious that the Hagia Sophia still holds her presence after all these centuries—after the long progression of emperors, patriarchs, and sultans and the new wave of tourists holding smartphones above their heads instead of candles and torches. The vast canopy of the inner basilica—like a gilded orange sliced in half—still demands jaw-dropping awe from all who enter.

Pendant chandeliers the size of giant wagon wheels illuminate the smooth stone floor. On the ceiling, a mosaic of the Virgin Mary, babe in arms, overlooks the tourist crowds, next to a series of giant calligraphy pendants with the name of Allah and his caliphates painted in gold (the Hagia is refreshingly grand enough for two deities to cohabitate in peace). And, in a charming mix of sacred and profane, a band of Hagia Sophia cats was holding court on the stones where emperors once tread (one in particular, a devout, cross-eyed tabby named Gli, has a large Twitter following and can often be seen posing for tourists and warming his paws in front of the altar lamps).

I left Jeff sketching the coronation floor in his notebook beneath the chandeliers and walked the stone arcades alone, paying my respects to the sheer tenacity of a hallowed space that endured after more than a millennium of on-and-off again collapse. Falling apart was as much a part of Hagia Sophia's identity as anything else. Her domes had been burned and collapsed; earthquakes had shaken her foundations; she'd been pillaged and plundered; everyone from Roman Catholic crusaders to Ottoman janissaries had battened down her doors. Even now, iron scaffolding covered half the southern wing, another ongoing, valiant attempt to prop up her sides. And yet—after all that falling apart—she was a force to be reckoned with.

I knew a kindred spirit when I saw one.

. . .

Why did you fall apart? That's what everyone had wanted to know—the gray-haired doctor, the therapist who coaxed me to breathe from my belly, my patient-but-worried parents. But, at the time, there was no tangible smoking gun. There were no geological fault lines or invading crusaders I could point to and say, *there's the culprit.* The only warning signs were the fine mental fissures that appeared after college graduation. I'd graduated at the top of my class only to find myself floundering in the housing crisis along with most of my peers—an early indication that nothing was guaranteed, even for "nice girls" who played by all the rules.

Maybe I fell for a twisted American exceptionalism—one that subconsciously assumes that life is naturally meant to be a comfortable upward affair, free from anxiety, forehead wrinkles, and bad credit scores. Falling apart was, in part, a reaction to the disturbing realization that life is not a hardy, invincible force that politely molds itself to hard work and human will. Life is threaded through and through with a great fragility. I noticed it in the softness of a baby's skull, the thinness of my great-grandmother's wrist, the wilting droop of a plucked flower—even the air I sucked into my lungs was a fragile cocktail of gases.

Everything is one snip, one puncture, one stab, one handful of degrees away from annihilation. And none of it makes much sense. You can get axed in a war over the gooey black remains of petrified plankton or by a bomb detonated in the name of invisible gods no one has ever actually seen or by a violent rebellion of your own tissues and cells. Everyone is a spark of aliveness in a temporary cage of bones. Nothing is certain. Nothing remains stable long enough to turn it over in your hands and hold it close against your heart. The entire universe—from cells to stars—is embroiled in wave after churning wave of change.

Most members of the American middle-class are able to rationally process these self-evident truths and continue sipping their iced chai lattes in relative peace. For some reason, I could not. The question of how—and why—I ought to proceed in the face of fatal chaos was not a question I could solve with a philosophy textbook or a Valium prescription. It was a physical question that nested in my ribcage and wrapped a hand around my gut. It was a possession. I was like Mohammad immobilized on the mountain, unable to take another step forward.

It was also an embarrassment. When someone asked, "Why are you falling apart?" I couldn't admit to struggling with mental illness. I didn't have terms to describe my utter inability to control my own body. I couldn't come out and say, "Oh, you know, I'm feeling paralysed by the human condition and I don't know what to do except curl into the fetal position like a frightened pill bug."

Wasn't everyone else managing to clock in to life despite that persistent little twinge of mortal dread? As a white American woman, I had privileges that so many others lacked. I didn't face racism or bigotry. I wasn't forced to marry against my will or work grueling hours in squalid conditions. I had health insurance and the security blanket of my parents to fall back on. So, why was I sitting near comatose on the lawn chairs in my parents' backyard, swaddled in blankets, staring blankly at the fence? To collapse under the weight of an existential crisis was, in some ways, to suffer a disease of affluence, to be able to afford the relative luxury of panicking over my own existence.

When friends asked, "Why did you fall apart?" it was easier to just shrug my shoulders and say, "I have no idea."

. . .

"We've got company," said Jeff. At my urging, we were leisurely eating pretzels against a tree on the sunny grass promenade that stretched between the Hagia Sophia and the neighboring Blue Mosque. A half-wild street dog was loping directly towards us across the lawn. It was a big Kangal with wet fur and a jaw full of sharp incisors. Half-wild Kangal dogs—with their pale coats and velvety black masks—freely wandered through the many parks and avenues of Istanbul. They were descendants of an old Anatolian sheep-herding breed. For the most part, they seemed friendly, though we'd seen a few facing off with the Hagia Sophia trash collectors in what appeared to be a longstanding feud.

"Probably wants a bite of pretzel," I said, tensing as it loped towards us, tongue lolling to the side. But I was wrong. The Kangal was wholly uninterested in the pretzel. Instead it nosed Jeff's hand and then curled onto the patch of grass beside his legs. Not a minute later, a second dog bounded over to join the pile and then a third, a dark lab that rustled its head under Jeff's arm, begging for a scratch. The dogs were indifferent to me. They wanted Jeff.

It was like a rumor of an old friend in town had rippled through the ranks. By the time the last bite of pretzel was gone, we were ringed by a mangy circus of half a dozen street dogs. Some stretched out catatonic in the sun, others were nipping sharp teeth at ankle fleas, and still others were rolling in the grass, angling their matted undersides for attention. Tourists walked by, mouths agape. Someone snapped a picture. An astonished Turkish kid yelled, *"Be careful!"*

I couldn't decide whether the sunbeams and snapping jaws were magical or alarming (an oft-repeated motif, as of late). This was the sort of surreal scene that only materialized when Jeff and I came together. Jeff would never have slowed down long enough to sit under a tree. I would never have attracted a cadre of mangy street dogs.

"What are you, Jack London?" I gasped. "This is completely bizarre."

He shrugged his shoulders and scratched the black lab's ears. "What can I say? Street dogs know a comrade when they see one. I'm dirty, I eat everything in sight, I don't care where I sleep, I intuitively read strangers, and I live shamelessly in the moment."

Twelve velvety Kangal ears perked as I lifted my hand to run my fingers through his unwashed hair. "Hey, do you believe what Mohammad was saying last night? That if you take a risk and move towards whatever it is you're drawn to, that the 'universe' or 'god'— or whatever you want to call it— somehow collaborates?"

He thought for a moment. "Well, a collaborative universe can't be proven empirically. But, to me, it doesn't really matter whether it's true or not because life is just more interesting when you let go and chase the draw—even if it doesn't make a whole lot of sense. I dunno. What do you think?"

"Something like that," I said. "I can't get away from the

idea that wonder is inextricably married to risk. Like even right here, we've got these dogs all around us, and it's magical, but not entirely safe. Wagging tongues next to sharpened teeth."

"And what is it about wonder that we all want so bad?" asked Jeff.

"I think it's when you're stopped in your tracks by the unfamiliar," I said. "You're coming face-to-face with something impenetrable that fundamentally transcends what you know about the world."

"Hmm," he smiled. "Unfamiliar and impenetrable. Sound like classic hallmarks of risk. Not that I know anything about that."

"Oh yeah, you're Mr. Play It Safe," I said, elbowing him. "But it seems like there's always that juxtaposition."

"I'm pretty sure that's what Mohammad was getting at," said Jeff. "Magic happens when you head out into the unknown with wonder in your right hand and terror in your left."

CHAPTER 4 | The Space Between Us

The bride was a vision of gauzy, cotton-candy pink from the top of her silk *hijab* headscarf down to the hem of her lacy gown. In her left hand she raised a bouquet of rainbow balloons up towards the Istanbul sky: red, orange, yellow, green, and blue. The groom, in suit and tie, beamed beside her, his arm crooked around her waist, holding her close. Aside from the brackish scent of fish, they'd practically stepped out of a fairy tale.

Jeff and I were standing on Galata Bridge with Mohammad, his friend Ali, a tall, shy Iranian, and Ali's girlfriend, Leyla, an Azerbaijani woman with a tempest of dark curls that nearly swallowed the sunglasses set on her head. Galata Bridge was the famed crossing from Old Istanbul to the newer Beyoglu neighborhood located north across the waters of the Golden Horn. (Though, in a city as old as

Istanbul, "new" has to be qualified—Beyoglu became a trendy Istanbul suburb back in the fifth century, when plows were just starting to become a thing.)

Along the bridge railing, old men with fishing poles crowded over the edge, sending their lines down into the Golden Horn, which—true to its reputation—was beginning to ripple gold in the afternoon light. Every block of cement was saturated with the pungent smell of nervous squirming bait, smoky fried mackerel, and fresh caught sardines. Taxi drivers muttered through bumper-to-bumper traffic and tourists angled around bait buckets for panoramic shots of Istanbul. The stunning backdrop also attracted newlyweds, who wouldn't be able to smell a mackerel sandwich for the rest of their lives without thinking of wedding photographs.

Jeff saw the magical cotton-candy bride right as I did. His eyes lit up. "Whoa, we should ask if we can take a picture with them."

"Can we not?" I pleaded. I hated imposing on other people—especially on their wedding day.

"Hey, it never hurts to ask," said Jeff, who had considerably fewer qualms about inserting himself into the immediate environment. Leyla saved him the trouble by skirting past us and over to the couple. After a short exchange, the bride nodded her head and Jeff ushered me forward, brushing my protestations to the fish-stained sidewalk ("It's fine. They don't mind!").

Without even realizing it, we were constantly tugging each other back and forth across lines of comfort and habit. He pulled me out of my safe observational tower and down into the sparkling chaos of the world, and when the chaos went too far, I pulled him up to consider the view from my tower. It was a perpetual negotiation. A delicate balancing act. Two tightrope walkers, arms outstretched, learning each other's rhythms on a tautly quivering rope. When we managed the balance, magic ensued. When we leaned too far into our own extremes, everything fell to shit.

In this case, the final result *was* magical. The bride and groom were smiling in the middle, a rainbow of balloons overhead. Jeff and I flanked the couple on either side like bookends. On a whim, we'd taken a similar side-by-side photo back at the Houston departure terminal—the two of us standing five feet apart, shoes together, back straight, eyes ahead like statues. The theme, which contained all the whimsical precision of a lost Wes Anderson clip, had immediately become a *thing*.

We'd repeated the pose with the Iranian bikers, in front of the Hagia Sophia, on the deck of a Bosphorus ferry, and next to the guy selling red Atatürk banners in Kadiköy.

If anyone asked why we were standing so far apart, Jeff either said it was a hipster artistic statement or made some quip about forgetting to put on deodorant that morning. I couldn't argue that the side-by-side green dress/red pants shots were visually striking. But I also suspected the space between us served a secondary, unspoken purpose—one that had nothing to do with deodorant or hipster aesthetic. From the very first date, our lightning-fast intimacy had been counterbalanced by a strict lack of definition.

Jeff was obsessed with freedom of movement like some people were obsessed with fantasy football lineups or organic kale juice. "I don't know what this is or how long it's going to last, but I don't want to box it in," he told me the week we met. He wasn't shy about expressing fierce affection, but it was always with the understanding that our connection was a nameless, living, breathing thing happening *right now*. There was no guarantee that it would exist in the same form the next day or even the next minute.

I'd never met someone so committed to existing unencumbered in the present moment. He kept his passport on his person at all times—just in case. He rarely mentioned anything beyond the next twenty-four hours, including his academic career or how he envisioned squeezing a house into a dumpster. If pressed on specific plans, he inevitably deflected with, "we'll see," as if the mere naming of future potentialities might somehow reduce the number of paths available (a cardinal sin in his book). On the nights he spent at my place, he followed the Cub Scout credo and left no trace behind in the morning. In his mind, even a cheap Crest toothbrush was a tether—a symbolic object that linked him to me, thereby exerting some infinitesimal press of obligation.

He hadn't always been this way. Before his marriage he'd been a serial monogamist with a handful of formal girlfriends stretching all the way back to high school. He'd always been independent, but this present compulsion towards freedom was a relatively new phenomenon, a variation on the traditional mid-life crisis. He was a pendulum, swinging away from wedding rings and house payments and into the exploratory realms. Our decision to form an experimental partnership governed by a single statute—to do what we truly wanted to do—wasn't just new territory for me. He was a fledgling, too.

The arrangement put us firmly in the ranks of a new generation of romantics who turn down the formal dating of ye olden days in favor of a lower-stakes "hanging out." "Hanging out" is defined by casual non-dates likely to take place with a cluster of other casual interests hovering around in the digital background. This new milieu of ambiguity offers unprecedented freedom and choice, but it also comes with an unprecedented level of anxious head scratching. It isn't uncommon to find modern romantics scouring texts, tweets, and Facebook timelines for any hint of where they stand in the murky, liminal space between "friend" and "girlfriend" or "boyfriend." (The "m" word—marriage—is typically reserved for ironic jest. Tying the knot is *so* last century.)

For Jeff, the leap to no baggage and no plans was actually quite small. Our unfettered travel experiment was just a slightly more extreme take on his life back home. Traveling with a single pair of cherry-red underwear wasn't radical. Jeff's radical act was traveling with *me*: a minor commitment, a potential tether, another body with opinions, needs, and desires to be taken into account.

The only other person in the universe who could make a legitimate claim against his freedom of movement was Sibel, his five-year-old daughter. She was the only one who heard the words "I love you" come out of his mouth. Jeff had partial custody, which meant that every other weekend he cleared his schedule and drove seven hours from Brownsville to College Station to spend a few days with her. He was protective of his daughter (I was the only one of his post-divorce interests he'd nervously introduced her to) even as he occasionally struggled to navigate the responsibilities of part-time parenthood. One couldn't switch gears at a moment's notice with a five-year-old in tow.

I enjoyed the two weekends I'd spent with Sibel out on his parents' farm. The fact that Jeff was a father had never bothered me. His preoccupation with freedom didn't bother me either—at least not at first. After a two-year hiatus from normal society, I was mostly open to anything. My only objective was to translate the expansiveness of my inner recovery back out into the physical world. Jeff was just the ticket. Our openness was an exhilarating challenge. And didn't his fingerprints match the secret "what-I'm-looking-for-in-a-man" document I kept hidden on my hard drive?

Like his, all of my past relationships had also fit the traditional mold. Strict monogamy. I love you. Let's (maybe) do forever. All of them had died slow, excruciating deaths. Partly because I was young. Partly because the thought of waking up next to the same person for a lifetime sent shivers down my spine. If a bond felt too confining—too limiting—I either abandoned ship or proposed an avant-garde open relationship that required staggering acrobatics (quasi-breaking up while quasi-dating, while quasi-seeing other people). Both routes inevitably led to the same crash-and-burn end.

With Jeff, though, I had all the openness I could handle. And then some. The same freedom he demanded for himself, he rigorously extended to everyone else, including me. He truly wanted me to do whatever I wanted to do—whether it meant abandoning ship or dating a different OkCupid guy every night of the week. This was an experiment. We'd just have to test and see.

. . .

Gulls floated above our small party as we reached the other side of the Galata Bridge. Leyla took the lead from there. Beyoglu was her neighbourhood. She lived nearby in a flat shared with a dozen rescue cats. "This way," she said, purposefully shepherding us across a busy intersection and into an underground tram station, where we boarded the historic Tünel car, which existed solely to cart pedestrians up and down a steep 600-meter hill. Leyla was in her mid-thirties with red-lacquered nails and an oversized handbag with the words "be loved" embossed in gold. She seemed a little shy with her boyfriend Ali, who was tall and dark-haired, with biceps that strained the sleeves of his T-shirt. He was shy with her too. I caught him studying her with devotion, like he still hadn't quite memorized her wild curls or the way she pursed her lips in a guarded smile. They stood next to each other on the tram like it was a second date.

"This is Istiklal Caddesi," announced Leyla, as we exited the tram station at the top of the hill. "Very famous street. Millions of people. Day and night." The station opened into a brightly lit pedestrian highway lined with old neoclassical buildings and a hectic array of boutiques, cafés, pâtisseries, bookstores, and nightclubs. Haughty mannequins looked out over a sea of pedestrians—some walking with shopping bags, many more walking with ice-cream cones. The United States was mostly missing this tradition of the promenade, where people walked to simply bask in the spectacle of the city.

Two weeks earlier, the street had been flooded with ten thousand peaceful protesters who were rallying against restricted democratic rights, media censorship, corruption, and police violence. Leyla told us her street had been foggy with tear gas. We walked past a splintered GAP display window and a group of protesters peacefully surrounding a candle-lit memorial to those who had recently been injured and killed. I stood in firm solidarity with the protesters, but felt a little hesitant about touring a cosmopolitan space that had so recently been the site of violent police crackdowns.

Leyla wasn't hesitant at all. This was her neighbourhood. Protests may have rocked the city, but they didn't detract from her pride. She wanted to show her streets off to us. I felt lucky to be seeing Istiklal through her eyes, though I was also distracted by sharp pain as we strolled down the cobblestones. After a paltry two days of walking, my lower back was already in bad shape. The topic of footwear seemed almost too trifling to mention after our grave discussion of the protests, but there was no getting around the fact that my peachy strapped sandals had been a huge miscalculation and Leyla would know where to get a more practical pair.

She shot into action when I finally pulled her aside. Ali, Mohammad, and Jeff were promptly dismissed. "I know a place," she reassured me. She said the words so firmly I imagined she already had a pair picked out and waiting on the counter. Within minutes we were standing in the middle of a busy, two-level shoe store. I used the opportunity to lightly pry as she combed the aisles, holding up a slew of sandals she thought would match my dress.

"So, how long have you known Ali?"

She blushed. "We meet one month ago on the tram."

"He really likes you," I said. "It's sweet."

"Yes, it is good," she said. "But also very hard. Ali does not speak Turkish. I do not speak Persian. So . . . we practice English together."

"Hold on," I said, incredulously. "So, when you two met, you didn't even speak the same language?"

"Yes, that's right," she said, placing a pair of brown wedge sandals into my hands. "We take lessons online and practice on the phone. Love is a good teacher, you know?"

I was floored. Dating was enough of a labyrinth when both parties could converse in the same language. I couldn't imagine having to navigate the nuances of attraction with a beginner's vocabulary. *How are you? Where is the bathroom? The weather is very warm today. (By which I mean to say, when I see you walking towards me my heart catches in my throat and I forget my own name.)*

Jeff and I were fortunate enough to speak the same

language, though we'd run a different gauntlet to find each other. Online dating wasn't for the faint of heart—especially in Austin, Texas, where dating is practically an unofficial sport. Competitive romance is inevitable in a place where half the population is single and, in certain ZIPs, everyone tends to look like a highly attractive twenty something even if they can remember the Carter administration.

Fresh-eyed university students bond over tofu and quinoa salad at the Whole Foods flagship. Cafés hang strings of soft, hazy lights at heights scientifically calculated to enhance facial features. You can spin around with your eyes shut and no matter where you stop, you're guaranteed to be standing in front of a quirky date spot with '80s sing-alongs or cocktails handcrafted from absinthe and egg white. The city practically begs you to fall in love or, barring that, to catch a show at Stubbs with some intriguing stranger you just met online. In Austin, opening an online dating account is a single's rite of passage. Serious contenders go for Match or eHarmony; lower-stakes lovers gravitate towards OkCupid; and the hookup crowd heads to Tinder or Grindr.

Since my last few years had been limited to a dysfunctional shuffle between my tiny studio, my therapist's couch, and a part-time filing job, it seemed prudent to go with the casual dating route. I signed my soul over to OkCupid, hoping, not for a soul mate so much as a decent reason to put on lipstick.

I saw myself as damaged goods, which made crafting the perfect dating profile a lot like doctoring a résumé to disguise a long unemployment gap (I'd done that, too). When prompted to describe my interests, I went with Japanese tea kettles, watercolour painting, and backgammon instead of disclosing my fondness for online anxiety forums, self-help books, and contemplation on the nature of being. I uploaded the one post-recovery selfie that didn't remind me of a ghost, I avoided mentioning my close brush with institutionalization under the "What's the most private thing you're willing to admit?" category, and by the time I finished, Clara Bensen almost seemed like the kind of girl you'd want to flirt with over Prohibition-era cocktails.

Profile complete, I nervously clicked "Browse Matches" for the first time. "What are you looking for?" OkCupid prodded. I didn't have an ideal man in mind, though I tended to click with academics—professors in particular. Curious, I restricted the search parameters to straight, single men with a PhD, age 32 to 50. With one click I was staring at a catalog of hundreds of men. The neat rows of profile pictures looked eerily similar to a shopping site. I randomly clicked on the first profile. "Mac-Dave" was a dark-haired scientist with Italian sunglasses and a suave complexion. His favorite book was *"Angles" and Demons* by Dan Brown and his most private confession was, "Im a Greek Mythical Sturdy Centaur." I rolled the proverbial eye. Were those acute "angles" or obtuse? *Sorry, Centaur Boy.*

Next up was "WinterNight," an attractive 39-year-old with dusty, windswept hair, a pensive expression, and a philosophy doctorate. My heart quickened. Maybe we could discuss Kierkegaard's thoughts on *angst* late into the night? Or maybe not. I scanned the summary of his ideal date, which had a higher word count than his recently completed dissertation. WinterNight's dream girl was hot, physically fit, smart, intellectually curious, honest, humorous, sweet, sensual, well-cultured, well-travelled, and able to follow a rousing philosophical conversation with a massage. In bed.

"Epic nervous breakdown" was noticeably absent on his list of required qualities. *No-go on WinterNight.* I clicked back to my search results and continued to voyeuristically scan through the academics until my mouse hovered over "one_man_tent," a slyly grinning Waldo in a crowd of studious faces. He even had the requisite black-framed glasses and a Mexican mariachi bowtie lined with candy cane stripes.

One_man_tent looked more like a prankster than an academic. He listed ramblin' and two-steppin' as his primary skills and claimed to spend his Friday nights "wandering in the chaos and manifesting the void," which seemed like an ambitious weekend hobby. He admired Diogenes the Cynic and spent his time thinking about coincidence, mortality, and the space-time continuum. *I like strange people*, he wrote. *Free people. People who don't fit the archetypes. People with unique pasts. People seeking and watching for something ELSE.*

Here was a man who spoke my language, and, as an added bonus, I didn't have to be one of WinterNight's sweet-n-sensual *Bachelorette* contestants to qualify for an email exchange. *People with 'unique' pasts may apply.* I fired off a quick message:

> *Dear Tent Man,*
>
> *Diogenes just happens to be my favorite ancient Greek dude. I have to admire any philosopher ballsy enough to renounce all his worldly possessions and move into an*

oversized barrel in the centre of Athens. It probably took several additional balls to mock Alexander the Great to his face. Opa! It's nice to know some of us can make a career out of upending social norms. Anyhow, just wanted to let you know that I also spend a lot of time thinking about mortality, coincidence, and the space-time continuum. So, yeah, my name is Clara and there you have it.

I panicked as soon as I hit send. Had I followed proper flirting protocol? Why did I open with a dead Greek guy? Who (besides Neil deGrasse Tyson) mentions the space-time continuum in an inaugural online dating message?

But the panic was needless. One_man_tent wrote back at 11:06 the next morning. His name was Jeff, he had a housing "situation" similar to Diogenes, and he wondered if I might have any interest in stirring up the pot of social conformity.

. . .

Leyla ended the night by leading the five of us to a small café positioned right on the edge of a steep hillside that overlooked a vast panorama of Istanbul. Mosque lights blinked in the glittering city nightscape and faraway boats glided through the water like phosphorescent fish. We never would have found the view on our own. She led us to a table and smiled. "You like it?"

We settled into chairs, reverently sipping little cups of *çay* like we'd just been handed exclusive tickets to the city's performance. Under the table, my feet were thrilling to the feel of soft new leather sandals. I left the original pair back on Istiklal, a gift for a passerby who had fewer miles to trek.

At the end of the table, Mohammad and Ali were catching up in hushed Farsi while Leyla sat across from me sharing pictures of her twelve cats on her phone. ("This is Koposh and Bobik. This is Noor and Findik under the blanket. Caco I found in the street.") Jeff flashed me a quick smile. He was sitting quietly beside me. We weren't touching.

We were both comfortable with independence, but Jeff was especially so. Even his OkCupid username—*One_man_tent*—hinted at his desire for space. Every aspect of his life was unconsciously designed to make it prohibitive for another person to fit into the picture. Dumpster house. Illegal office dwelling. Break-neck travel across the world.

And yet we had ended up together, attempting a risky tightrope act—attempting to connect without any expectation about how long the connection would last. We were testing whether it was possible to love without grasping;

to let space exist between two bodies without reaching to tighten the gap or pushing to widen it; to hold nothing back; to wholly offer our love with no guarantee that it would take the same form tomorrow as it did today. We were trying to hold each other lightly, firmly.

CHAPTER 5 | Pink Ring

It takes nearly twelve hours to get from Istanbul to Izmir, a large, sunny metropolis on the western coast of Turkey. First, you take a three-hour ferry across the Bosphorus to the coastal town of Bandirma, where you rush out of the port and down to the nearest *shawarma* joint for a slapdash lunch. Then you board an eight-hour train to Izmir. In retrospect, it's easy to forget how much of travel is spent gazing—not at jaw-dropping monuments or museum exhibits—but out the dusty, scratched windows of boats, buses, planes, and trains. Travel is a constant state of suspension in spaces that are neither here nor there, but somewhere in between.

There's as much to be said for these long, monotonous stretches of movement as the destinations themselves—particularly on trains, where the acres of flashing farmland, the low, clacking waltz of the carriage, and the faint mirage of your own reflection in the window all conspire to lull you into a hypnotic state of wandering reflection that rarely occurs in the busy humdrum of ordinary life. In her personal diaries, Sylvia Plath likened the language of train wheels to a mental rhythm, "summing up moments of the mind like the chant of a broken record: god is dead, god is dead. Going, going, going. And the pure bliss of this, the erotic rocking of the coach."

I was content to be lulled by the erotic rocking of the coach for all eight hours of the trip, but Jeff was different—he had to move within the movement of the train. The seat next to me was often empty. I imagined him swimming laps up and down the length of every car, studying the passengers, hoping for a reason to start a conversation. Occasionally I'd open my eyes and find a small, bird like offering beside my chair, a packet of chocolate wafers, a juice box, or a flimsy paper cup of coffee with one sip missing. He was, as before, completely unruffled by the idea that we were arriving in Izmir at 10 p.m. with no place to stay. "We'll see. We'll see," was all he'd say.

We'd mutually decided on Izmir over a traditional Turkish breakfast of flatbread, tomato, cucumber, and goat cheese. We chose it simply because it looked good on the map

Jeff kept in his pocket: a large, sunny metropolis perched on the western coast of Turkey. Never mind that "large, sunny metropolis" captured the sum total of our knowledge about the place or that we'd fired off a few online Couchsurfing requests to potential hosts in Izmir, but hadn't stuck around in Istanbul long enough to check our email for replies. Once again the end of the line was unknown. It was still unsettling.

We arrived to a pitch-dark station. The landing platform was deserted. Jeff and I stood in a pool of light under a streetlamp and stared at each other without even bothering to say, *What now?* Then, as if on cue, a bike manifested out of the shadows, gliding past us from stage left. The bicyclist circled back, a wild girl-sprite on wheels.

"You must be Jeff," she said, pointing to Jeff's Stetson. "I recognize the hat from your Couchsurfing profile." Jeff's eyes were as wide as mine. We weren't exactly sure who she was out of the many hosts we'd emailed or how she'd intuited our exact arrival at the station when we hadn't known ourselves. "My name is Ezgi," she said amiably. "I got your Couchsurfing request. You can stay on my couch."

And that was it. We were no longer lost.

Ezgi was a pixie with dark hair that curled like wire springs around her face. Big, brown owl eyes peered at us from above her handlebars. She was early twenties, but her psychedelic flower pants and loud, plastic jewelry gave her the aura of an old soul hippie child. "It's Friday night fever!" she crowed. "Let's go!"

We followed her through empty plazas and boulevards, hopping from streetlamp to streetlamp, glowing islands in the dark. She pulled into a corner shop for a couple beers and then led us to our final destination, a wide, grassy promenade along the Aegean. The promenade was filled with entangled lovers, fortune-tellers selling prognostications, and cliques of kids scattered across the summer lawn (Izmir was the Venice Beach of Turkey, according to Ezgi).

Her friends were in one of the jolly piles on the promenade lawn. They were caught up in a match of Go (an ancient Chinese strategy game I associated with old, bearded men, not hip Turkish kids). We slipped off our shoes and easily settled into the rhythm of the group: beer, weekend plans, and skinny sunflower seeds shucked between teeth. It was nice. Informal.

Something about the lull of the Aegean waves and the tangy malt of Turkish beer put Jeff into a particularly relaxed mood. After an hour or two he tipsily leaned over to Ezgi and requested to borrow one of her plastic rings. It was huge. A glittery pink plastic thing that looked like it had been lifted straight from Barbie's jewelry box. Garish ring in hand, he leapt to his feet and pulled me with him. He was about to create a scene. I could feel it.

Still, I didn't expect him to drop to one knee.

Ezgi and her friends whooped as he dramatically kneeled and slipped the pink ring on my finger. *Will you marry me?* It was obviously theatre. An act. Another crowd-pleaser. And yet, when I said *yes,* and he swung me backwards and planted a deep, drunken kiss on my lips, I surprised myself by feeling a spark of something that wasn't entirely pretend. It was a tenderness that verged on longing, which wasn't allowed. I brushed it off like a wayward spiderweb. *Don't think I'm taking your name, baby.* A joke for a joke. The crowd laughed, drunk on warm sea air and beer.

. . .

The glittery ring was still on my finger when I woke up on Ezgi's living room couch the next morning. I was wearing one of her T-shirts, an oversized tangerine thing that perfectly matched the psychedelic riot of her flat. Ezgi's apartment looked like a class of kindergartners had supervised the task of decorating. The foldout couch was covered in loud, retro flower sheets. A hand-painted koala bear mural stared sleepily across the living room, where an army of plastic toy figurines was carefully arranged on every flat surface. (Other notable décor included a prominently placed SpongeBob SquarePants poster and a fluorescent alien in a gas mask.)

The tangerine T-shirt also matched the ring. I twisted its gaudy, jelly-like form around my finger. The previous night's engagement scene had been an intoxicated joke—a bit surprising given our mutual avoidance of anything even vaguely commitment-related—but a joke nonetheless. Neither one of us had the slightest interest in walking down the aisle. We'd both made that clear. And yet, I felt the same surge of longing from the night before—not for till-death-do-us-part, obviously, but for a shred of what the ring represented. A few slender boundaries within our undefined expanse. The hope of steady companionship. The intention to remain connected beyond the next five minutes. *You're breaking the rules,* I told myself. *You aren't supposed to want this.*

Jeff was banging pots around in the kitchen. He was incapable of making a cup of coffee at anything less than maximum volume. His red pants were still strewn on the floor, which meant he was gambling that the pot would brew before Ezgi woke from her summer mattress on the balcony. Sure enough, he emerged from the kitchen, half-naked, holding a cup of Nescafé in front of his belly button. I caught him eyeing the ring. He had hawk eyes. His commitment radar was swirling with bright crimson flashes. *Red alert. Red alert.*

"Still got the bling, huh?"

Busted.

"Oh," I said nonchalantly. "I guess I fell asleep with it on." I casually slipped the ring off and surrendered it to the stack of empty Domino's pizza boxes that Ezgi ordered at 3 a.m.

He picked up the ring, still warm from my finger, and lightly twirled it around in his palm. "I swore I'd never remarry, yet somehow I'm on the coast of Turkey, engaged to a woman who hasn't changed her clothes in five days." Another joke.

I laughed awkwardly, "So, should we change our Facebook relationship status to engaged?"

He said nothing. I said nothing. The room was still except for the low hum of street traffic drifting in through the open window. Our fake engagement was cumbersome in the sober light of morning. The ring was a symbol and symbols carry weight—even if they're dripping with pink glitter. The sight of the band unnerved him. He saw it as an anchor disguised with jewels. A constraint.

"Look, we've practically been conjoined twins since we left," I said, fumbling for an out. "Don't you think it would be good to go our separate ways for a bit?"

"Great idea," he said, agreeing a touch too quickly.

It was an awkward check. A tight jerk on the reins. We were shy cats, hesitantly moving towards intimacy, then springing back under the bed at the first sudden movement.

. . .

It didn't take long for the morning sea breeze to turn hot. My shoulders scorched as I walked along the ocean promenade. I was an animal returning to the water's edge. Or maybe just a glutton for punishment. After leaving Ezgi's flat I'd drifted back to the same patch of promenade lawn from the night before, though it looked different in the stark sunlight. Seaweed and empty sunflower husks baked in abstract piles on the hot sidewalk. The boardwalk was almost empty in the sluggish stillness of early afternoon. Old men dozed in their chairs. Women fanned themselves in doorways, angling for any hint of a breeze. I pulled my unwashed cotton scarf around my shoulders and continued walking towards the point where the promenade dead-ended into a rough industrial pier.

Walking solo is different from walking with a companion or a group. As a lone, anonymous walker, you are both guide and observer—responsible for setting your own route, pace, and orientation to the possibilities of the urban landscape. And, if the solo walker has a distinct orientation to the city, so does the city, in turn, to the walker. Any experienced traveller knows that the likelihood for spontaneous exchanges between strangers is much higher for a solo pedestrian than for those locked in the less penetrable bubble of a pair or a group (where an off-the-cuff conversation might be interpreted as an unwelcome interruption).

If Jeff and I had been walking together, the wiry old fisherman sitting under the cluster of scrubby, ocean-battered trees probably would not have unfolded a plastic chair and invited me to share his triangle of shade. (There is the matter of walking solo as a woman, which tends to invite a different experience than walking solo as a man—whether in Austin, Texas, or Izmir, Turkey.) At first, I was wary—conscious of my aloneness and the isolation of the boardwalk. Correct protocol was to avoid eye contact and keep walking as if I hadn't heard. But for some reason I did look in his eyes. They were genuine. I glanced at his hands, too—they didn't seem to carry any propensity to wander too near my body. It was a gut thing: I sat.

There was no name exchange. To my delight we skipped the small talk and launched right into a proper discussion. The fisherman was trilingual. He had a sharp grasp of English (among other things), which he'd picked up in the U.K., where he and his now ex-wife had worked for years. ("A *witch* of a woman," he said, spitting bitterly into the wilted grass beside his bait coolers.)

"IS. THIS. FISH?" He was a Broadway performer mimicking sightseers in a singsong voice. "Bloody tourists. They ask me stupid questions in English. I pretend I'm a simple fisherman who can't understand their jokes until the very end when I say, 'Can I help you with anything else?'" He cackled wickedly. "Their open mouths are the only entertainment I can afford."

Stories sprang forth in wild, hopscotch jumps. He effortlessly segued from sly, semi-profound statements about the nature of life to crude epithets about his ex-wife. Every sentence—whether holy or profane—was laced with a dazzling helix of *bloody fucks* and *fucking hells*.

"You're in my *fucking* house right now," he said when I asked where he lived. In the mornings, he and his fishing partner dove for bait on the ocean floor, in the afternoons he set out the fishing lines, and in the evenings he unrolled his sleeping mat under the trees. All of his belongings were packed in a neat pile behind the bait coolers and plastic chair living room. Technically he was illegally squatting, but there was an arrangement with the police. He was surviving, but it wasn't easy. His wrinkles were starting to add up.

Some days he left the fish and went to the mosque to teach Arabic to Turks who wanted to read the Koran in the original language. "I don't give a fuck if you're Muslim, Protestant, or Catholic," he roared at the empty boardwalk like a prophet ministering to an invisible crowd. "It's all the same god. Doesn't matter who you pray to—the important thing is that you pray. I always say 'prayer is best, fuck the rest.'"

"That's a policy I can get behind." I laughed.

"What are you doing in Izmir?" he asked, abruptly hopscotching to a new topic. I gave him the gist of the baggage-less experiment, skipping over the part about online dating and my abstract relationship status. He responded with irreverent skepticism. "Why would a girl like you travel without a fucking bag?" *A girl like you. Rich, white girl.*

Someone who doesn't have to store her bed beneath a scrubby tree. He had a point. I felt a flush of embarrassment. My nameless companion lived off of bait worms and fish beneath a tree. His future was constantly uncertain. I was acquainted with a certain type of unfamiliarity, but not like this—not at such a precarious, bodily level. The thought didn't inspire me to go home and sanctimoniously blog about how I was forever changed by a brief brush with poverty. I wouldn't roll out the tired, count-your-blessings trope of how truly grateful I was *not* to be the penniless fisherman I'd never see again.

If I had spoken as freely as he did, I would have said: *I have no idea why I'm wandering around without a fucking bag, but I'm trying to listen deeply and watch closely and somehow piece together little fragments of what it is to be human—and you offer small clues with your fervent prayers, and your streams of obscenity, and the morning dives where you comb your fingers through the ocean floor, feeling for enough viscous worms to get you through the end of another day.*

. . .

Streams of sweat trickled down my calves as I stood alone in a hot field of stone columns and crumbling arches. It was sticky, but the torpid afternoon heat was a fair tradeoff for having a Roman agora entirely to myself. I'd spotted the Roman columns on the morning bus into the city from Ezgi's place—a crop of Ionic pillars anachronistically set between beige office buildings—and immediately decided I would make a solo pilgrimage to the ruins.

As a kid I'd exhausted the library's archaeology catalog, spending many a flashlight-lit night under the covers where I plunged the legendary depths of Troy, dared myself to look at Tutankhamen's cloth-wrapped corpse, and studied the scandalously exposed breasts of Minoan female fashion (while worrying God would find out). As a writer, ruins still drew me in—they're like rough outlines begging to be fleshed out with the scent of smoky campfires, ancient love triangles, and grisly plagues.

Ruins also appeal (somewhat morbidly) to my existential bent. They offer a decimating sense of scale against the backdrop of time. What better reminder of mortality and the ultimate conclusion of all human striving than to sit amongst the crumbled shards of civilizations that once held global top-dog status? "Beholding old stones, we may feel our anxieties over our achievements—and the lack of them—slacken," wrote the philosopher Alain de Botton. "Everything is, in any

event, fated to disappear. Judged against eternity, how little
of what agitates us makes any difference."

The agora ruins had been easy to find. I followed Ezgi's rough
map of Izmir away from the fisherman's home-under-the-
trees and through a series of relaxed, ordinary streets. The
fisherman promised coffee if I ever returned. *I might be poor,
but I can afford a bloody cup of coffee.* I shook his hand and
told him it had been a *fucking* pleasure. An hour later, I felt
a swell of satisfaction as I handed five lira to the short, graying woman in the agora ticket booth. I didn't need Jeff to get
around. I had no need of glitter pink rings.

My ears pricked as I wandered through jagged remnants
of the agora, which had been laid across the field like Lego
blocks. Water was running somewhere in the stones. It was
faint, but close. I followed the sound to a stone staircase that
led downward, away from the beating sun and into a labyrin-
thine cellar of mossy arches and narrow conduits that still
flowed with water. Not only did I have an agora to myself—I
also had a two-thousand-year-old Roman aqueduct.

I slipped my sandals off, drenched the back of my neck
with water and sprawled out in the moss. I would sit here
for the entire afternoon, I decided. Sitting silently seemed

to be a Turkish tradition. In Istanbul, shopkeepers stared languidly into the distance. No one moved to open a paper or check a phone. Yesterday, too, on the train, I'd seen old men standing, hands behind back, alone on empty country roads, meditatively studying the horizon with (god forbid) no apparent purpose. Solitary, public contemplation was rare to my American eyes—limited to bus stops, art museums, and the homeless on street corners.

I was a master of solo contemplation, but not necessarily in a Zen, one-with-the-universe sort of way. There had never been a time when I hadn't contemplated furiously, in tempestuous cyclones of thought. Mental monsoons. Violent gales of rumination.

As a kid, I'd deliberated over the only thing I really knew: theological mysteries. *Why did my dad have a direct line to God, while I'd never heard so much as a holy peep? What happened to remote Amazonian tribes that never got the chance to learn the salvation prayer? If God was such a standup guy, then why was he sending all our neighbors to hell?*

My first existential crisis struck at the age of ten. I abruptly abandoned my faith in God after coming to the conclusion that his creation (the world) was, in many cases, rather unpleasant. Skepticism was a serious transgression for a pensive, religious kid who prayed before meals, spent summers at church camps, and worshipped in the pews every other day of the week. For months I bore the anguish of a godless world alone, instinctively sensing that my parents couldn't handle complex metaphysical doubt on top of putting food on the table, educating five homeschooled kids, and maintaining a strained marriage. Instead, I dropped hints at bedtime with casual questions like, "Dad, how do we know God is real?" which roughly translated to, "Dad, how do we know we're not just lonely, godless creatures struggling blindly through an uncertain life that's guaranteed to end in death?"

My parents did their best to expound on the finer points of evangelical theology, but the standard biblical narrative always required some degree of blind faith, which I found unsatisfactory. I was a criminal investigator who required hard evidence to close the case. Someone handed me a Christian apologetics book that claimed proof of God's existence based on fossilised chariot tracks in the Red Sea and old Hebrew scrolls in a cave. But even at the age of ten, I suspected the archaeological record wasn't cutting it where questions of the divine were concerned. I demanded rainbows like Noah and manna like Moses. I wanted to feel eternity shooting up my spine.

I didn't know it at the time, but my parents were unable to quell my existential doubts because they had yet to quell their own. In fact, I owed the entire fact of my life to an existential French play written in 1944. My father was a young architectural student at UCLA when he read *No Exit*, Sartre's famous one-act performance where three damned souls are locked in a room together for all eternity. The idea that life was an endless series of miserable and meaningless interactions ("Hell is other people," Sartre so winningly put it) so disturbed my father that he put down the play and headed straight to the nearest church to sign up for heaven.

It was there, in Los Angeles, that he met my mother, who was also searching for hope in the house of God. After giving birth to my sister Anna, she'd spent the last few years working as a massage therapist to support my sister and herself in a tiny Venice Beach apartment. Oddly, she too was drawn to the church by way of Sartre—in her case, his novel *Nausea* was the motivating terror. They were married in a small ceremony. My mother wore a white straw hat with flowers. My dad wore big glasses.

I was born in Portland, Oregon, a year later—an anxious, colicky baby brought into the world in part via the unsatisfied mind of an existential philosopher. Sometimes I joke that I cried because I already knew I would have to pick up where my parents left off. Every parent hands down genetic propensities for various traits (green eyes, clinical depression, a thick gut in middle age). My birthright just happened to be a load of existential doubt.

. . .

"There's another American guy here. He's wondering if you'd like to join him for a drink," said Ezgi. I was sitting in the bohemian Spanish café where she worked. Jeff had agreed to meet me there around dinnertime. Dinnertime for the Izmir crowd was, apparently, much later—the rustic wooden tables were mostly empty. *Where was this mysterious American?* "You can't see him from here," she said. "He's sitting around the corner." Her owl eyes flickered. *Come on!*

"Okay," I said. "But how does he even know I'm here?"

She glided away in her black harem pants without answering. I followed in her polyester wake, curious. Today was a day for accepting invitations. I turned the corner and there was Jeff, smiling his joker smile. Of course he was the mystery American. I should have known. "We split up for a couple hours and you're already agreeing to drinks with strange men?" he said. Ezgi giggled as he pulled me towards him at the table. "I missed you," he whispered softly without a trace of the morning's awkwardness.

That's how he was. Tension was always followed by a silent split. Then he'd show up a few hours later as if he'd forgotten about the offending incident altogether. Speaking anxieties into the air—giving them audible weight—was an act of vulnerability. Safer just to skip it and move on. If he opened to me, I might do the same to him. And then where would we be? It wasn't so easy to "keep things simple" with our underbellies exposed.

"Do you hear that?" I cocked an ear towards the street. It sounded like faraway chanting. Ezgi floated by with a pitcher. She said there was a protest a few blocks over. It wasn't just Istanbul that had been engulfed in political protests. Seven million people in over forty Turkish cities had rallied against authoritarianism over the last month, Izmir included.

"We've got to see this," said Jeff.

"As long as we stay out of the way," I warned. I flashed on a memory of the photograph that made the rounds on the TV networks the week before we left—a riot policeman firing tear gas directly at a Turkish woman in a red dress. She was casually holding a purse, her eyes downcast, her posture dignified, relaxed, like she had been noticing a lost coin on the ground when the gas sprayed her hair into the sky.

My parents had expressed concern before Jeff and I left. Up until a few months ago, I'd been a frightened hermit surviving on a diet of peanut-butter-jelly sandwiches and protein shakes. (My mother admitted that she still took a deep breath whenever she saw my number calling.) The thought of me flying across the world with someone I hardly knew was a bit nerve-racking, but headlines shouting "Downtown Istanbul a Battle Zone" and "Thousands Across Turkey Protest Erdogan's Autocratic Style" made the whole proposition even harder to swallow. To her credit, my mother mostly kept her worries to herself. "Just be careful," she sighed. "Having five nomadic children is probably my karma for taking off when I was eighteen."

Jeff also had a history of making his parents nervous with his choice in travel destinations. There was a tense run-in with the Kyrgyzstani border patrol, a camp site in the remote Wadi Rum of southern Jordan, a walk through a rough Cape Town neighborhood, and a twenty-minute chase in a rental car along the Kalahari desert in northern Namibia. His Facebook profile had a photo of him standing in front of the Sea of Galilee with four Hasidic Jews in wide-brimmed black hats, smiling, thumbs in the air. "They were hitchhiking through the West Bank," Jeff said. "I gave them a ride. They said God would protect us."

Jeff's dad always said, "Son, maybe you could go to Hawaii this year."

I wasn't afraid of political activism—I'd marched with Occupy activists in Dallas and studied colonialism and the history of struggle in developing countries—but the protests in Turkey were another order of magnitude. It didn't feel appropriate to insert myself into the middle of someone else's movement. If I had any role, it would be to stand in quiet solidarity with the hundreds of protesters pulsing down the main corridor, giving witness as their fists punctured the sky, Turkish flags overhead.

We walked over, chants increasing in volume with each step. The collective dissent was riveting. It was a rare, thunderous thing to hear—to physically feel—an assembly of voices hurling the same words into the air, again and again. I'd heard communal voices raised in song by church choirs and at a Radiohead concert, but never on this scale. Never with so much force and necessity.

I turned to share the moment with Jeff, but he was gone.

The crowd had swallowed him. Apparently, the "wading into the chaos" line on his OkCupid profile was meant to be quite literal. I was alone again. I wasn't afraid, so much as annoyed. There was nothing to do but thread along the edge of red-clad protesters, scanning for a Stetson as the marching throng swept me block after block. Ahead, the sun was setting over the Aegean. *Goddammit!* For the third time in twenty-four hours I was moving back towards the seaside promenade, back towards that same little patch of love-struck lawn.

I felt a rise of irritation by the time the protest reached the sea. The Stetson was nowhere to be seen. *Is he aware of anyone else in the universe except himself?* I refused to chase after someone who took off without notice. I wasn't a man hunter. I wouldn't let myself care.

But then, just as I decided to give up and make my way back to Ezgi's café, I saw him striding towards me, eyes creased with worry.

"What happened?" I yelled. "You disappeared!" I was in his face. Hackles raised. Eyes flashing.

"I don't know!" he said apologetically. "One minute I saw you and the next I didn't. I've been looking everywhere for the last half hour."

"Oh, is that right?" I said sarcastically.

He held my shoulders at arms length and looked into my eyes. "Yeah. *It is*. Did you really think I would just leave you?"

I did, in fact, assume he was capable of just leaving. The uncertainty between us was so carefully preserved that I wouldn't have been entirely surprised to see him toss the glitter pink ring into the Aegean and ride off into the glow of the Izmir sunset without looking back. And yet, he was staring at me so tenderly, as if a vanishing act was about as likely as teaching penguins to fly.

In a complete reversal of our morning cat dash, he had come out from under the bed and was rubbing against my legs, purring sweetly. Once again he was a pendulum undulating back and forth between freedom and desire. I was doing my best to follow the swings—to carve out space for them, to explore where I myself fell on the spectrum—but I couldn't handle the vacillation indefinitely. At some point he'd have to decide what he wanted. And so would I.

CHAPTER 6 | The Oak Tree

It was a slow-motion moment: Jeff reached for the sesame pretzel on the table in front of us. He tore off a bite and deftly chomped it. I could see the horror unfolding, but I was powerless to stop his molars from moving up and down, grinding the bread to pieces. My eyes were big round saucers. I rammed my elbow into his ribs.

The pretzel wasn't ours.

It belonged to the diminutive Turkish grandmother sitting across from us on the train to Ephesus. She had a floral scarf tied around her chin. Her two granddaughters sat beside her—hands neatly folded under the table, eyes as saucer-wide as mine. No one uttered a sound. We stared at each other in shock, like we'd just witnessed a robbery by a thief who hadn't bothered to run.

Jeff was forever nibbling. At restaurants, he would reach

for a dash of guacamole, a furtive handful of french fries, a sly finger in the hummus bowl. Once, back in Austin, a bachelorette party left a restaurant table still laden with half-eaten croquettes, champagne, and charcuterie plates. He brazenly ushered every bottle and plate over to our table, citing "upcycling." ("It's a matter of reputation! How can I call myself 'Professor Dumpster' and let all this go to waste?")

I furiously elbowed him again. "Oh my *god*. Jeff, you just ate her pretzel right in front of her! We are now the American oppressors who snatch bread right out of the elders' hands."

"Shit. I thought it was the pretzel *you* bought!" he whispered. He turned and gave the grandmother an apologetic bow followed by a profuse entreaty for forgiveness. Without saying a word, she slid the stolen pretzel back to her side of the table like a chess piece across a board. I froze, waiting for some sort of public scolding, but instead she simply tore off a second piece of pretzel and ceremoniously presented it to Jeff, her face breaking into wrinkled sunbeams. The famous Turkish hospitality had absolved him of his pretzel sin. The two girls giggled shyly as he popped the bite into his mouth and tipped his hat to the grandmother.

"What American stereotype are you going to pull next?" I whispered. "Khaki shorts with a fanny pack?"

. . .

We were on our way to the ancient ruins of Ephesus after an early departure from Ezgi's apartment in Izmir. We'd left her asleep in her open-air nest on the balcony where, earlier, Jeff had tiptoed to retrieve our clothes, which were hanging on the drying rack after their first proper wash of the trip. Before the trip, friends asked us what we planned to wear when our clothes were drying. We admitted we had no idea, but—like everything else—we planned on improvising. Improvisation, in this case, was Jeff wearing one of Ezgi's old towels loosely draped around his nethers. Mostly naked myself, I'd crouched in the window and photographed him trying to slip on his red underwear without dropping the towel and scarring Izmir with the sight of his cojones blowing in the breeze.

This was the odd intimacy of Couchsurfing, a digital tribe that encourages floating in and out of strangers' lives (occasionally in underwear). More conservative travelers tend to shy away from the potentially life-endangering act of logging onto a website, browsing a catalog of local hosts, and sending half a dozen emails requesting to snore free of charge on a perfect stranger's couch. There are safeguards, of course; both hosts and travelers are screened, reviewed, and rated (a fairly effective mechanism for filtering out the creeps). Beyond that, Couchsurfing tends to be largely self-selecting. Only a certain genial type of soul is willing to open her home to strangers. Conversely, only a certain type of traveler is amenable to taking shelter on a stranger's couch—risking awkward personality clashes, late-night pizza deliveries, thin walls, and couches that exude *eau de cat*.

The sacrifice of privacy, however, is rewarded by the rare chance to experience a foreign place through the lens of someone to whom it isn't foreign at all—someone who knows the history, the shortcuts, the slang, the secret overlooks, the cheap-but-hearty cafés, the best salutation for drunken toasts in local bars. With a Couchsurfing host you rarely end up at the Eiffel Tower, the Statue of Liberty, or any other tourist landmark with a postcard rack (and if you do, it's usually to observe something behind the scenes).

Couchsurfing is like peering into lit windows at night—a quick, intimate glance into another person's interior. It's distant and personal at the same time. I knew nothing about the city where Ezgi grew up, whether or not her father had a temper, or what she secretly hoped for when she climbed into bed at night. Yet, I'd slept in her pyjamas, depleted the world's beer supply with her band of friends, and basked in the fluorescent glow of the alien mural on her front door.

To invite a stranger into your most private space is a radical act of trust—one that tends to compress traditional relationship arcs into an ultra-concentrated couple-day span. Some hosts prefer polite small talk, but it's just as common to skip the niceties and dive straight into the subjects travel guidebooks recommend avoiding at all costs (mainly the taboo realms of politics, religion, and sex). With zero preamble, Couchsurfing conversations can wander from local politics to intimate family memories to accounts of steamy hookups in foreign lands. (Jeff once met a Couchsurfer who tallied all the countries she'd had sex in using her fingers and toes; she had to count each hand and foot twice over.)

Ezgi's couch embodied the surfing experience. A brief, immersive local experience. No scheduled itinerary. No concierge. No flag-wielding tour guides. Just a red couch beneath a giant koala bear mural (and a washing machine, thank god).

. . .

We made up for the former lack of flag wielding tour guides amidst the colossal ruins of Ephesus. They materialized from behind ceremonial columns and commemorative plaques, expounding on Greco-Roman history to breathless crowds that glistened with sunscreen and sweat.

Ephesus was indeed breathtaking—a vast marble jungle gym of temples, baths, and amphitheatres rambling through acres of eucalyptus and palm-dotted hills. Efes, as the Turks called it, had traditionally been a thriving Greek outpost until the Romans showed up, bringing with them baths, aqueducts, and gladiators, which in turn gave way to crosses, apostles, and believers as religious tides shifted over the centuries (Ephesus is one of the seven churches of Asia mentioned in the New Testament and was visited by many of Jesus's disciples).

Unlike some American historical sites, there were few cordons separating tourists and their fingerprints from the cultural treasures at Ephesus. Almost none of the ruins were off-limits. I clambered around the spot where the Apostle Paul penned his letter to the Corinthians and up to the single remaining column of the Temple of Artemis, one of the Seven Wonders of the Ancient World. I crouched inside one of the cupolas of the jaw-dropping tiered Library of Celsus, which once held cupboards filled with twelve thousand scrolls (eventual kindling for a massive library fire in 262 A.D.).

Jeff and I naturally drifted apart soon after we entered the grounds. It was better that way; he could jog three laps around the entire complex in the time it took me to fully absorb one temple. I trailed a Chinese tour group for a while and then cut away towards an empty side path lined with dilapidated stone rooms. I ducked into a room with caving slab walls, amazed that it wasn't off-limits. Weeds sprouted from the cracks. Someone had left an empty cigarette case. I ran my fingers along the stones, imagining who might have sat in the room twenty centuries ago.

Turkey was full of biblical sites I'd studied as a kid. The Tigris and Euphrates rivers were linked to the Garden of Eden. In the east, Mount Ararat was rumored to be the final resting place of Noah's ark after the great flood. Many of the New Testament books were letters written either to or from Christian communities in Turkey. But as I touched the stones, it was hard to imagine any connection between the marble ruins of Ephesus and the vein of Christianity that I'd known.

In Portland, my brother and sisters and I had grown up during the Pentecostal revival movement of the 1990s. Church services were wild affairs that often ran late into the night. Ministers called down the Holy Spirit and laid hands on rows of churchgoers who toppled under the power like dominoes. It wasn't uncommon to see congregation members writhing on the floor in ecstatic states or running down the aisles praying in foreign tongues.

When my family moved to Fort Worth, we joined a megachurch associated with a popular televangelist. It was different, but equally surreal. There were rallies. Conferences in stadiums packed with thousands of followers. There was money, too. The pastors owned jets, motorcycles, and luxury suits. Film and audio crews broadcasted the sermons around the world. It felt like we were part of something big.

But the celebrity was also confusing. As a teenager in the youth worship band I'd often wondered what Jesus himself would have made of all the flashy pomp and circumstance. Would the carpenter from Nazareth be surprised to see the complex religious structures that had laid claim to his teachings? Was this the message of the gospel?

The evangelical church wasn't part of my world anymore, but now, with distance, I didn't begrudge the fact that it had shaped me. My upbringing was a strange window into searching and desire. It set me on an unusual trajectory. I'd grown up watching a community of believers fervently struggle to connect with something bigger than themselves.

The execution was often dogmatic and deeply flawed, but the individual desire for divine communion was true. The church offered a toehold of certainty in a "fallen world." It offered a god to cry out to, firm rules to live by, and the promise of an end to suffering. I, of all people, could see the appeal in that—even if I was no longer a believer myself.

. . .

After my meditation in the ruins, I found Jeff in the Grand Theatre, a cyclopean amphitheatre carved into the side of a hill. He was (predictably) onstage—the epicentre of the mostly empty twenty-five-thousand-seat theatre where Roman gladiators once bludgeoned each other to a bloody pulp. I sat several rows back, bracing myself for whatever form of entertainment he appeared to be preparing. (At least it didn't involve bludgeons.)

"Class, today we're going to discuss spatial variability of intra-urban particulate air pollution!" he bellowed across the stadium. In the front row, a tourist couple peered quizzically from beneath a sun umbrella. *Was this some kind of historical reenactment?*

"Or we *would* be discussing it if any of you slackers had enough discipline to show up to class this morning. Are my lectures *so* boring that 24,900 folks decided to sleep in for a NOON lecture? I'm taking a letter grade down for every ass not in a chair. No excuses either. I'm pretty sure your 'grandma' isn't still 'trapped in a freak pillar collapse.' If anyone has questions I'll be holding office hours over in the Temple of Hadrian."

It was a ridiculous performance, but even so, I laughed. He could coax a smile out of me faster than anyone I knew. My friends wondered (frankly and aloud) how someone with my temperament could handle his blithe and shameless wildness. What was I getting out of this experimental arrangement? I struggled to explain that, in defiance of all logic, his cheery madness was often the very thing that calmed me. It was a swift antidote to my anxiety and I drew on it, wonderingly. "As far as I can tell, he's genuinely happy ninety-eight% of the time," I told my mom over the phone. "I've never met someone like that."

When I woke up with my head in a tangle, he rarely tried to dissect my intangible worry. Instead he gently wrapped me in a cocoon of blankets, straddled my body with his knees, and rocked me back and forth with an infectious grin on his face. After a few minutes of rocking, the anxiety inevitably lifted in a fit of giggles. He had the rare ability to summon me out of some dreadful, fictional future and back into the physicality of *right now*—a space that was always manageable.

. . .

"Do you know the legend of the seven sleepers?" I asked Jeff. We'd collapsed under the needled shade of a pine tree after witnessing enough hewn marble to fill a dozen museums.

"Nope," said Jeff, wiping beads of sweat off his forehead. "What's it about?"

"Well, it involves time travel. I overheard a tour guide telling the story. Apparently the Ephesians were way ahead of Doctor Who."

According to local lore, in 250 A.D., a group of seven young Christians fled to a cave in the hills above Ephesus to escape religious persecution. After their first cave slumber party, the seven sleepers sent one back down to the city on a reconnaissance mission for bread. Strangely, that person found that the anti-Christian city had been adorned with crosses overnight. The sleeper questioned a local shopkeeper, only to discover that it was no longer 250 A.D., but the early fifth century and the Roman Empire had been converted to Christianity. The seven sleepers had slept, not for one night, but for 180 years. The plot twist was so unbelievable that all seven sleepers promptly keeled over in shock.

"God, that would be so surreal," I said. "For us, it would be like going to bed before the Civil War and then waking up to smartphones, frozen pizzas, and silicone boobs. Time is such a weird thing."

"I don't believe in it," Jeff declared, as if time were an Internet conspiracy theory. "Or, at least not in an arrow-straight line like we assume. I think it's fluid and cross-dimensional. We just haven't figured out how to model it yet."

"That's why you're so obsessed with coincidence."

"Yeah, coincidences are like tiny peepholes into time and causality and the connections between things. Almost everyone experiences coincidence—odd little synchronicities. Sometimes there are big synchronicities, too. A bizarre confluence of factors that are tough to logically explain."

"Right," I said. "But if you hypothesise that time isn't necessarily unidirectional and that causality might be able to reach back and work in reverse . . ."

He finished my thought, ". . . then you've got a whole new set of potential explanations for how and why objects intersect in time and space."

"Like the oak tree."

"Yeah," he smiled. "Like the oak."

. . .

The oak tree appeared the very next morning after our first Capitol date. It was the first Saturday of April. Bright redbud trees had overthrown the watery gray palette of winter. The pungent, oniony smell of daffodil bulbs wafted down the street, a reminder that this was the only time of year when one could walk barefoot through a patch of grass without fearing a skirmish with fire ants or spiked sandburs. Windows were carelessly opened. Doors were left ajar. The entire population of Austin was flocking outdoors to appreciate the newly temperate conditions.

Giddy from the night before, I too was compelled to dig up my sandals from the back of the closet. I abandoned my studio and drove to the Greenbelt—the lush eight-mile stretch of limestone forest on the far western edge of Austin. In the two years since I'd moved to the city, I had only been to the Greenbelt once. On my first visit the creek was dry, but this time it was swollen with spring rain. I waded in up to my calves and shrieked as my toes went numb and my arms prickled with gooseflesh.

I left the water and stumbled down the trail like a drunkard heading nowhere in particular. I was delirious from meeting Jeff and the surging creek and the bright shocks of green rupturing out of every branch and crevice.

I saw the tree a mile or two in. It stopped me dead in my tracks: a mammoth oak in a clearing a little ways off the path. The trunk was thick as a caravel mast—and at least a century old. Its branches snaked into the sky, waving me closer. The tree was pulling me into its orbit. I unbuckled my sandals, approached the gnarled roots and made a full rotation around the base, feeling for footholds in the bark. I would climb the tree—it felt more like a command than a choice.

I wasn't a teenager anymore, but after a few calculated lunges and a scraped knee I was up, cradled in a cathedral of branches. Breathing. Bark against skin. Moist dirt between my toes, under my fingernails. No one around. A holy moment.

I drove home and thought nothing of it. Jeff came over the next morning. Our second meeting. I didn't tell him which of the sixteen porches in the apartment building was mine, but he strode up to my open door and walked right in like he'd lived there all his life. The ramshackle pile of seashells on the porch gave it away, he said.

He was wearing an olive-green 1940s Air Force jumpsuit that he'd pulled out of a dumpster behind a resale shop on the Mexican border (like most of his stories, it sounded like a Texas tall tale, but was probably in the general vicinity of the truth). The jumpsuit was an outrageous outfit for a science professor—or really anyone not in the Air Force—but he was enormously proud of it. I couldn't deny that it suited him as we stretched out on my floor rug and studied each other, testing whether the magic from two nights ago was still around without the aid of tequila. He pulled out his phone.

"You wanna go for a drive? Yesterday I found this place I want you to see," he said. "I think you would really dig it."

"Sure," I smiled. "Where is it?"

"It's this place called the Greenbelt. You ever been?"

I hesitated. "Actually, I was there yesterday."

"Really? Well, I'd only been once before and I hardly remember because it was a skinny-dipping party at 3 a.m. after too many beers. Anyway, this time my friend and I hiked a long way in and we found this giant oak tree way down in the woods. You have to see it. It's *insane*. Like, it reached out and grabbed me." He stretched his arms out across my rug to mimic the branches.

I sat up and studied him. *Was this some kind of weird stalker prank? Maybe online dating had been a mistake.*

"Well, that's pretty strange," I said. "Because I found a

tree, too. And I climbed it."

"Huh, weird," said Jeff. "I climbed my tree, too. You wanna see a picture?" He punched around on his phone and then held it up to my face. I froze. There was the exact same oak tree with all its tangled limbs. *My oak tree.* I stared at Jeff, struck mute. *Was this a trick? Had he followed me? Where was the camera crew hiding?*

"You're not going to believe this, but that's the exact same tree I climbed yesterday," I whispered. "What are the chances of that?"

Ending up at the same park on a Saturday afternoon was somewhat reasonable—the Greenbelt was popular within Austin's 250 parks. Hiking the same section of the eight-mile route was also possible. But the sequence started to become less plausible with the oak tree itself. What were the chances that both Jeff and I would gravitate off the same trail, on the same afternoon, towards the same tree—one of hundreds of old oak trees in the Greenbelt? And then, even if we were drawn to the same tree, what were the chances that we would both feel compelled to *climb* it within hours of each other? I hadn't climbed a tree in years. Neither had he.

It was also surprising that the tree impacted him so deeply that it was the first thing he mentioned when he walked into my house the next morning. I was a botany geek, but I had never walked into someone's house and said, "Oh my god, you're never going to believe this new cypress I found down by the river."

Jeff and I stared at each other. The photo of the tree lay between us on the rug. "Does this mean something?" I asked.

"I don't know," he said cautiously. "Meaning sort of implies that someone or something is out there consciously orchestrating events and I don't think that's how causality works." He ran his finger along my arm, playing dot-to-dot with my freckles. "On the other hand, something unusual is definitely going on. When these inexplicable synchronicities pop up, I think it's a reminder to pay very close attention to whatever is going on."

"Look, when we met two nights ago, it felt like . . . " I trailed off, hesitant to be so forthright with someone I'd just met. Every dating columnist ever employed by *Cosmo, Glamour,* and *Marie Claire* would unanimously vote against the words I wanted to say.

"Like what?" he prodded. "Just say it."

"It felt like something was stirred up," I said. "Something big."

"Well, I can definitely confirm that," he winked.

"Oh please. Spare me the throbbing member jokes. The feeling wasn't even particularly romantic. When we met, I dunno, it felt like a cloud of potentialities was suddenly unleashed. Like, our meeting activated something. Woo-woo, I know, but I think there's something between us. Something magic."

Instead of looking alarmed, he smiled. "I think you might be right. And, hell, I like a woman who isn't afraid to start a second date with a declaration of cosmic connection."

CHAPTER 7 | Greek Expectations

The moment Jeff and I agreed to bid *gulë gulë* to the Ephe-
sian ruins and "sail" to Athens on a diesel night ferry, I con-
jured up half a dozen scenes from the first half of *Titanic*:
moonlit waves, dolphins at the starboard bow, and a sharp
sea breeze that vitalized the lungs without ruffling the hair
(basically, all the opulence minus the iceberg). I don't know
why I did this. I was breaking my own travel rule by projecting my imagination on a foreign place before I'd actually
seen it. Reality so rarely—if ever—aligned with my fantasies
that it seemed safer to do away with expectations altogether
and hold out for the element of surprise. "Oft expectation
fails, and most oft there where it promises," warned William
Shakespeare.

Perfectly fulfilled expectations require either an
extraordinary degree of control or an extraordinary degree

of luck—neither of which is guaranteed on the road or, really, any other situation in life. Plus, in addition to being statistically unlikely, perfectly fulfilled expectations are boring. We assume that we, in our infinite wisdom, are capable of imagining the best, most optimal outcomes for ourselves, but as it turns out, unfettered reality and unexpected detours are often the very things that force us to come into our own.

Still, even knowing that, the *tendency to expect*—to predict, to surmise, to forecast—is strong. It's practically hardwired into our DNA. There's nothing wrong with future forecasting, obviously—it clearly has a place when it comes to practical stuff like train schedules, hurricane conditions, and 401(k) accounts—but there's a shockingly short mental leap between the practical and the fantastical. One minute you're rationally planning your summer herb garden and the next you're fantasising about fictional ferries or what you'll do when your job is outsourced to Chennai, and your boyfriend runs off with that flirty, tattooed bartender, and you succumb to what is almost certainly a rare form of cancer, based on the WebMD forums you've been combing for days.

The human mind never ceases to amaze with its ability to construct events, people, and experiences that—whether good or bad—quite literally don't exist any place except in a web of synapses. My gilded-age ferry fantasy was shattered as soon as we walked up the boarding ramp of a vessel whose interior looked more like a Boeing 747 than an Olympic-class ocean liner. There were rows of airline-style seats with drab upholstered armrests and narrow cubicle bathrooms with overflowing trash cans and floors slick with god-knows-what. I never found the Grand Staircase with its polished balustrades or the vintage sleeping bunks with the neat little privacy curtains.

For entertainment, the night ferry did offer a series of open decks, but not the kind where you stand at the helm and spread your arms while Leonardo DiCaprio whispers, "All right, open your eyes." If you opened your eyes you'd see clusters of chainsmokers flicking used butts over the railing. Alternatively, if decks thick with tobacco fumes weren't your thing, you also had the option to relax inside in front of the dozens of overhead television sets playing Greek soap opera at volumes clearly intended to accommodate the hearing impaired. The current episode featured a chiseled Greek businessman haranguing a weeping debutante with inky streams of mascara running down her face (maybe the Greeks invented tragedy, but plot twists have clearly gone downhill since Sophocles married Oedipus off to his own mother). I sighed as we settled into our designated seats. My chances of achieving REM state on the night ferry were about the same as spotting a moonlit dolphin at the starboard bow.

Jeff and I were both tipsy. We'd gone through a respectable number of beers while waiting at the docks and the combination of alcohol and exhaustion made the night far more amusing than it actually was. Jeff pulled out his notebook and jotted a methodical line of check boxes down the page. "Time to assess the first leg of the experiment!"

"What, *now*? It's midnight."

"Precisely," he said, adopting a clipped BBC radio accent. "Now, if you will kindly direct your attention to the following survey: any new acquisitions since experiment onset?"

"I guess just the sandals in Istanbul."

"Right-o. Last date of clothing wash?"

"Yesterday, at Ezgi's."

"Very good. Total number of washes since experiment onset?

"One."

"Current state of bodily hygiene?"

"A little earthy, but not like a French metro in July or anything."

"*Ex*-cellent. Total number of external rinses?"

"Umm. You mean showers? Every day, which I can't say for you."

He sniffed his armpit. "Getting a bit earthy, eh? Anyway, on to our final survey point: are there any items you do not currently possess but find yourself desiring?"

"Dolphins, industrial earplugs, and a therapist for the asshole on the soap opera."

"Let me clarify," he said. "*Requiring,* not desiring."

"Honestly? Right now the only thing I require is a tube of toothpaste."

Back at Jaime's house in Houston, Jeff had insisted that we didn't need to waste critical pocket volume on something so superfluous as toothpaste. Everyone had toothpaste, he insisted. It practically grew on trees. It flowed like minty milk and honey in the streets. He stubbornly stood by his claim even when nary a tube of minty paste was to be found in Mohammad's flat in Istanbul. Ezgi's psychedelic abode might have had toothpaste, but we couldn't tell the toothpaste apart from the bevy of other vials and tubes in her bathroom. The risk of buffing foot cream into our molars seemed high, so once again we brushed with water and kissed with lips firmly closed, hoping the lingering whiffs of *doner kebab* wouldn't spell an onion-flavored end to our nascent romance.

Still, Toothgate aside, the pitfalls of minimalist travel had also failed to live up to my expectations. As long as my clothes didn't smell gamey, I hardly noticed I was wearing the same outfit on repeat. I took daily showers. My armpits smelled like lavender. My underwear was clean. In short, I was a far cry from the sweaty, dirt-caked, beer-stained vagabond I'd prophesied when Jeff first brought up the idea of traveling "light."

I wasn't suffering in the least. Of all the items in the world, a travel-sized toothpaste tube was my sole object of desire. I hadn't given a second thought to cardigans for cool nights, Gore-Tex windbreakers, evening formal wear, hiking boots, patent heels, or the half-dozen skirts I always packed but never got around to wearing.

It's a rare thing to step into the extraordinary lightness of wanting nothing. Despite having more physical resources in my 380-square-foot efficiency than any of my ancestors had accumulated since the dawn of humanity, the number of times I could claim to be totally satisfied with the sum total of my possessions was alarmingly few. Desire was an insatiable beast. Yet by eliminating the possibility of new acquisitions from the outset, I'd moved into a surprising state of satisfaction with the basics: food and shelter shared with someone who made my heart beat a little faster. In a way, it was an alchemic process—by dropping desire, a cheap paper cup of Nescafé, a crocheted blanket on a stranger's couch, and a clean pair of underwear suddenly transformed into tiny, generous miracles.

. . .

If I broke my rule once imagining the night ferry, I broke it twice imagining Athens as a modern throwback to the Golden Age when Socrates sculpted the foundations of Western philosophy. I vaguely pictured draping robes, Olympians with prominently featured abs, olive branch crowns, and marble pillars at every turn.

I didn't actually expect the ferry crew to hand out olive wreaths like Hawaiian leis on a cruise ship. But any romantic idealisations I did have were immediately quashed as we stumbled sleepily off the boat ramp and into the teeming Athenian Port of Piraeus. The port cut a grim figure with its swooping harbor cranes, gritty steel *clank-clank* of chains, and the low, industrial drone of the ferry engine—all set against a smoggy, late-morning sky. There were no Olympian abs in sight.

The danger of basing impressions of famous destinations on postcards and brochures (or in my case, Hellenic pottery) is that postcards fail to set the surrounding context, which can range from picturesque to gritty to dreadfully mundane. You can get a stunning view of the Great Pyramid of Giza from a nearby Pizza Hut (built on top of a Kentucky Fried Chicken). You can admire the ivory curves of the Taj Mahal from the top of a rubbish heap. The *Mona Lisa* is not an impressive mantel-sized masterpiece but a modest 2.5'-by-1.75' portrait never surrounded by less than three hundred flailing tourists. The iconic Athenian Acropolis is at the epicentre of a smoggy world city, replete with a grinding blur of metro stops, graffitied walls, and urban commuters.

I wasn't prepared for the spinning sense of disorientation as we covered the few dank blocks between the Port of Piraeus and the nearest metro station. Jeff, in all of his narcoleptic glory, had passed out on the night ferry despite the blaring soap operas. I hadn't been so lucky.

We'd docked in Greece right as I'd begun to adjust to Turkey. I'd decoded the spiraling letters of the Turkish alphabet. I could order Turkish coffee a *little sweet* instead of *very sweet*. I knew how to thank the bus driver with a *teşekkür ederim* that didn't sound like a cat hacking up a hairball. But now, just as I'd caught my proverbial breath, we were starting the game all over again in a new metropolis with a new metro system and a new language with a new script that, to my tired American eyes, looked more like calculus than words. The disorientation was exhausting, and yet, I reminded myself, it was also what we had come for.

Jeff had successfully arranged a Couchsurfing host in Athens. Veroniki rang us up to her third-story flat, a sunny, spare set of rooms with a plant-lined balcony overlooking the Acropolis in the distance. She was mid-thirties with dark pensive eyes that matched the long hair she wore braided to the side. Her expression alternated between warmth and faraway reserve. When she laughed, a touch of melancholy tumbled out with the laughter. Jeff noticed it too, I could tell.

We collapsed on her minimalist cantaloupe-coloured couch and she settled, birdlike, into a chair. There were the usual preliminaries to cover: where we'd travelled so far, what had possessed Jeff to live in a dumpster, whether she enjoyed working as an English translator, and how she was faring in the tanked Greek economy. She ministered to the dark circles under our eyes with *freddos,* a distant relative of the cappuccino made with crushed ice and sugar in a tall clear glass. And caffeine. Scoop after scoop of dark jet brew.

"Drink slow," she warned. "It's strong."

It was only a few sips before I felt my pulse thumping in regions that didn't usually thump. My fingertips. My knees. The ridges of my earlobes.

"I usually go to a modern dance class on Thursday afternoons," said Veroniki. "You're both welcome to come along if you're not too tired."

"I'm afraid my skills don't extend beyond the waltz and the East Texas two-step," said Jeff. "But Clara does that modern stuff where you roll on the floor and pretend you're an earthworm or a gorilla or whatever."

"I don't know," I said, feeling my toes beginning to jitter in their sockets. "It sounds fun, but the ferry wore me out." I dabbled in modern dance back in Austin, but it was in a warehouse with a DJ and a hundred-odd vaguely New Age dancers who freeform rollicked and twirled for two sweaty, essential-oil-infused hours before sitting in a circle for a closing "*om*" meditation. I didn't know one chakra from another, but I liked the primal energy of dancing communally to no choreography but my own. Plus, the lack of formal choreography was critical for someone who could barely manage the Hokey Pokey.

"I'm a terrible dancer," I warned.

"Come on! There is no such thing as a bad dancer!" said Veroniki, toying with the end of her braid.

I took another sip of *freddo* and gave her a jittery smile. "Well . . . okay. Why the hell not?"

"This is so great," she said. "You're going to love it."

The dance studio was a couple stories up in a building overlooking an expanse of beige apartment blocks. In the distance, I could see a billboard with a Greek cell phone advertisement. Veroniki handed me a pair of stretchy dance pants and an eggplant-coloured T-shirt. "I won't tell anyone you cheated on your green dress," she smiled.

Jeff was gone. He'd briefly toured the studio before leaving to wander around the neighbourhood on his own. I felt a flush of relief as Veroniki steered me over to the dance floor and introduced me to the class—I was relieved that Jeff wouldn't be around to witness my impending humiliation. The class was made up of half a dozen young women and every single one looked strong and vital, like they could pirouette up the Acropolis without breaking a sweat. The instructor—a wiry, curly-haired man with eyes that went two different directions at once—spoke almost no English, but calmly assured me that dance was a universal language.

I nodded in agreement even as I identified all the exits in the studio.

It wasn't so bad at first. We luxuriously stretched our legs. We breathed into our centres. We rolled like timber logs to get acquainted with the floor. But any glimmer of survival was extinguished the moment the instructor had us leap across the floor like gazelles. Within seconds it was obvious I had more in common with a dyslexic sloth on opioids than a graceful gazelle. The instructor barked guidance, but I wasn't sure if his lazy eye was directed at me or Veroniki, who was elegantly leaping by the window. It was horrifying. *But, whatever.* I threw my pride to the polished dance floor and continued to pant my way through elaborate rolls and gliding gyrations. My bar for success was moving in some fashion that vaguely resembled the rest of the class—as in, I would not collapse inert on the floor while everyone else gracefully *chasséd* across the room.

After a brutal eternity, we finally took a break. Veroniki, who was an experienced dancer, leaned over, looking concerned, "That was the warm-up. Now the class begins."

If I were a cartoon, my chin would have quivered as a giant teardrop rolled down my cheek. The *freddo* was inducing chest palpitations, the curl ups had introduced me to abdominal muscles I didn't realize *Homo sapiens* possessed, and I was dangerously close to vomiting caffeinated beverage all over the dance floor. "Veroniki, I think I'm going to have to sit this one out," I whispered.

. . .

Veroniki put me at ease over skipping class. As we left the studio to meet Jeff, she patiently endured my self-conscious chatter about how I had difficulty judging left from right, how I was spatially impaired, how I'd nearly ruined my seventh-grade square dancing finale by wrapping my arm around my partner's pubescent waist and dominating the do-si-do. "Don't worry about it," she insisted with her forlorn smile.

If there was any cure for my damaged pride, it was the traditional Greek spread Veroniki ordered at the café where we met Jeff. It was early evening—the sun was just beginning to dip—and the red-checked patio tables were mostly empty, except ours, which was divinely heaving with spiced racks of lamb infused with lemon, cucumber salad, tangy Kalamata olives, wine, and enough hot bread to feed an army.

Between bites, Veroniki painted a grim portrait of modern Athens. "You won't believe this," she said. "The state just fired all university security guards who have not earned a master's or Ph.D. It's like a bad joke."

All of Greece was paralysed in an economic chokehold. Austerity measures meant that bankruptcy, unemployment, and draconian taxes were par for the course. Veroniki was fortunate. She had steady foreign translation work—unlike half of the younger generation who had no jobs at all. Jobs simply didn't exist. College graduates languished in their parents' homes instead of moving forward with traditional rites of passage. The most productive phase of life was indefinitely put on hold, a delay that depressed the psyche as much as the savings account.

I knew the feeling, at least a little. Any optimism I'd nurtured during my existential crisis was lost the moment I unpacked my clothes in my parents' brick house in the Fort Worth suburbs, in my teenage bedroom, in the chipped laminate dresser that used to house my glitter nail polish collection.

It wasn't that I was ungrateful—I was relieved to have family support—but I'd also crossed a definitive line in the sand. I was reluctantly joining the ranks of the Lost Generation, the title the national think pieces had somberly assigned to the swathe of broke, indebted Millennials who were camping out in their parents' basements, serving foam-leaf cappuccinos with anthropology doctorates, and endlessly trolling Craigslist for an entry-level personal assistant job that a thousand other qualified applicants were also sharpening their swords for.

I felt betrayed more than anything. My expectations had been reduced from optimistic reveries to a sorry pile of pencil shavings. I can't even say what the expectations were specifically, but I know they involved being easily successful in the same way I'd always been easily successful. *Profoundly entitled*, as the think pieces put it. One of the more widely touted pieces by Paul Harvey, a University of New Hampshire professor, opined that Millennials "have been led to believe, perhaps through overzealous self-esteem building exercises in their youth, that they are somehow special, but often lack any real justification for this belief."

If all eighty million members of my generation were actually guilty of profound entitlement, it's partly because we'd possessed the maddening nerve to believe the cultural messages we'd been spoon-fed since birth. *(You're unique! Follow your bliss!)* I comforted myself with the knowledge that at least my overblown perception of specialness had an altruistic bent. I was a dreamy idealist who came into the world with a built-in saviour complex. In college I enrolled in an international development degree, naïvely planning to dispense peace, love, and malaria pills in war-torn refugee camps. I would *make a difference, goddammit.* Then the housing bubble popped. The only work I could get after graduation was at a jewelry studio where I sold high-end wire working pliers to wealthy retirees in search of a new hobby. Peace and love were in short supply. I could barely save myself—let alone anyone else.

The fact that all my aspirations had culminated in jewelry pliers didn't exactly bolster my relationship with reality. I daydreamed about taking a torch to every inspirational poster ever printed with the phrase, "Do what you love. Love what you do." In what perfect universe did everyone just abandon their miserable jobs to survive on a diet of dreams and motivational quotes superimposed on photos of tropical beaches? Try telling the tired, uninsured Walmart checkout lady to "do what you love." I wanted to sneak into strangers' Pottery Barn–inspired homes and sadistically replace their framed *"Live, Laugh, Love"* posters with Cornel West's take on life: "We're beings towards death, we're two-legged, linguistically-conscious creatures born between urine and feces whose body will one day be the culinary delight of terrestrial worms."

I'd have saved myself some heartache if someone had informed me that life isn't a linear, teleological climb that culminates in some final plateau. It tends to look a lot more like a rolling tumbleweed that gets blown off arroyo cliffs and trapped in barbed cow fences just as often as it rolls smoothly down the road. I wish I'd known how many forces are completely out of our control and how often we fail to get exactly what we want (and the disappointment that sometimes follows when we *do* get exactly what we want). I wish I'd known to hold everything a little more loosely; to be more accepting of the millions of messy, glorious forms a single life can take; to quit acting like the human experience was a geometry equation with a firmly established, *correct* answer. And hell, I wish I'd known it's perfectly acceptable to have a little fun with the whole business of being alive.

But I wasn't informed. The prevailing cultural directive was: stay in school, follow the rules (and your dreams), indenture yourself with $40,000 in educational debt, and come out on the other side with a bright future and a basket full of gold stars. Expectations were high. So was the disappointment.

. . .

Veroniki said we'd take the scenic route home from the restaurant. With full bellies and moods mellowed with wine, we wandered down a pedestrian walkway bustling with tourists, families, and vendors selling knickknacks. The old neighbourhood of Plaka—an undulating maze of cobblestone staircases, plazas, and narrow alleys—lapped at the base of the tall, rocky promontory where the Parthenon sat, overlooking Athens like a gleaming crown against a violet-navy sky. "This place is called 'Neighborhood of the Gods,'" said Veroniki.

In the hush of early evening, it felt as if the gods had banished exhaustion and mangled gazelle leaps, finally wooing us into the gritty dreamland of Athens. Like living embroidered lace, pink bougainvillea and grapevines with green filigree curls traveled across terraces echoing with the clink of wine glasses, over trinket shops selling terra-cotta busts, and up whitewashed walls and bright shutters.

Past and present were all mixed up. For every modern taverna serving olives and vine leaf wrapped *dolmades,* there was an old agora column popping out of a patch of overgrown grass. Cheap souvlaki joints churned pop radio across half-excavated archaeological sites. I looked around, half-expecting to see Dionysus running out of a *raki* bar with a bottle of wine and a throng of nude hedonists at his side.

Jeff slid his arm around my waist and pulled me close as if to say, *Isn't this magic?*

Veroniki gave us the eye. "You guys are too much." She said it like a joke, but there was that same sadness I'd seen before. It surfaced again back at her apartment when she handed Jeff boxers and a T-shirt that said *Coca-Cola* to borrow while our clothes were in the wash. Jeff giggled his high-school-girl laugh as he pulled the T-shirt over his head. His belly button was popping out. The elastic boxers barely contained his waist.

"Oh my god. I look like Winnie the Pooh," he said.

"They were my ex-boyfriend's," said Veroniki from the kitchen. "He was small."

Jeff gave me a look. *Ex-boyfriend's pyjamas?* He pressed her for more, unable to resist piecing the puzzle together. They'd been together for six years. There wasn't any fundamental problem. It just hadn't worked out. "I loved him," she sighed, standing in front of us, slightly lost in her own living room. It cut straight to my heart the way she said it. *I loved him.* Totally exposed. Tender yet resigned.

We said good night to Veroniki and curled up on the foldout cantaloupe couch. Jeff switched off the lamp and promptly began to snore, but I laid awake, wondering if her words would come out of my mouth someday. I'd never considered deeply *missing* someone. I was a leaver, a free spirit who jumped into relationships even when it was blindingly obvious they wouldn't last. There were endless options, weren't there?

Jeff made me nervous. Of all the men I could have messaged on OkCupid, the unpredictable wild card was the one I wanted to stick around? My feelings had begun to coalesce into something that bore an alarming resemblance to that forbidden four-letter word. My love was built with big things—he accepted me in my entirety, he was kind, he never turned anyone or anything away, and he could make a killer margarita—but the small things mattered just as much. I loved the way he woke up in the middle of the night and sleepily whispered, "What are you thinking about?" into my ear. The way he always reserved the last bite on the plate for me. The way he tore crude hearts out of recycling paper and arranged them by the bathroom sink.

He was racking up reasons for me to care about him, but that didn't mean he was safe. Loving him was a risk. Wanting him to stay was dangerous. Wants are one step away from expectations—and everyone knows what those lead to.

CHAPTER 8 | Wanted! The Outlaws

The folksy twang of Merle Haggard and Willie Nelson serenaded us awake in Veroniki's dark, pre-dawn living room. Jeff had set his morning alarm to "Pancho and Lefty" the night before. It was my favorite outlaw ballad, but not at 5 a.m.

I moaned at Jeff from under the pillow I'd pulled over my head. "Am I being woken up this early because I killed a bunch of orphan kittens in a former life?"

"Trust me," said Jeff, who was already gathering our clean laundry from the drying rack on the balcony. "The only way to experience the *true* essence of the Acropolis—or any tourist mecca—is to show up right as the sun rises. It's not the same once the cruise ships dock and three thousand tourists are all trying to post the same shot of a Doric column on Instagram."

"You do know the Parthenon is filled with industrial cranes, right? Aren't you worried the scaffolding is going to impinge on your purist essence?"

"Please? I promise it will be worth it." He cheerily dropped a pile of wet clothes on top of my blanket-covered body. "Sorry. They're still damp, but I'm sure they'll be dry by the time we beat everyone to the top of the Acropolis."

"I read somewhere that 'Acropolis' translates to 'highest city,' which, interestingly, in the Ancient Greek can also be interpreted as, 'no-way-in-hell-I'm-running-up-a-500-foot-stone-mountain-before-sunrise.'"

He was completely undaunted. "That's fine. I'll just meet you at the top."

The Acropolis ticket booth opened right as the light turned a smoggy gray-gold. It was a quiet scene. A few groundskeepers were checking trash bins and stocking vending machines with water bottles. The ticket booth operator sleepily handed us our tickets and pointed us over to the entrance, where a few other early birds were waiting for the gate to be unlocked. Jeff stretched his legs like he was training for a triathlon. When the gate finally opened, he shot past a surprised American family and took off down the path, a damp red blur disappearing into the olive trees.

I followed behind, stubbornly refusing to climb up the stone escarpment any faster than a brisk walk, which was fine because in the end, we reached the staircase leading up to the monumental colonnades of the Propylaea at exactly the same moment. Hiking up a steep limestone path worn smooth by six millennia of sandals required more skill than either one of us had anticipated.

The Greeks knew how to make an entrance. The immense stone staircase rises up to meet imposing walls and a copse of towering columns that are so thick even the shadows seemed to carry weight. The sheer number of steps gives visitors plenty of time to meditate on their own smallness before they pass under the Propylaea and into the Acropolis.

The Acropolis itself is equally striking—a dusky plateau of marble where temples spring out of stone—though the Parthenon is the one everyone comes to see. Even as a skeleton with scaffolding wrapped around its giant Doric bones, the Parthenon dominates the Acropolis grounds. Athens surrounds the jutting promontory in every direction, an ocean of roofs glinting in the gauzy morning sunlight.

To protect against earthquakes, the Parthenon's fluted

columns were bowed ever so slightly inwards—if they continued on, they would eventually meet a mile into the sky. It was good foresight on the part of the Greeks (who built the temple in a mere nine years). The structure was an architectural masterpiece—and we were witnessing it alone. Jeff stood in one of the sharp triangles of sunlight filtering through the Parthenon columns. He was jubilant. "Isn't this worth it?" I nodded, not quite ready to concede the spectacular view or the fact that, for a few short minutes, we'd had the entire Acropolis to ourselves.

"It's pretty incredible," I said. "Hard to believe it only took us a couple weeks to upgrade from OkCupid to Plato."

"Well, I did pay for the premium account," he said, slipping his arm into mine.

We stood, side by side on the front porch of the Parthenon, peering up at the Ionic friezes in a suspended state of awe (*Where were we? How had we gotten here? Where was this heading?*).

Like all moments, it didn't last. The sun was pressing into our upturned faces. Jeff was fiddling with the camera on his phone. The magical state of awe was shockingly fleeting. Ancient stone friezes could only compete with the demands of the present moment for so long (eventually a rumbling stomach, an ankle blister, or the desire for a Parthenon snow globe wins out).

"It's funny," I laughed. "One second you're thinking, *my god, I could stare at this hunk of marble forever and never fully appreciate it* and the next you're thinking, *oh man, I could really go for a hot dog.*"

"Looks like we're not alone in that sentiment," said Jeff.

Morning cool had quickly shifted to summer swelter. The mesa of pale marble refracted heat against the clusters of tourists panting through the Propylaea with their walking sticks, water bottles, and weighty Nikons. Done with our short, self-guided tour, Jeff and I sat on a bench under one of the only trees in sight. He tugged his still-wet red underwear out of his pocket and set them to dry as we settled in for our second round of entertainment.

"One point for every person who takes a picture of a cat, pigeon, or squirrel, as they stand in the birthplace of Western philosophy," I said.

"Already up to five," said Jeff.

"Two points for every kid who doesn't give a flying fuck about the Socratic method and would rather play in the dirt."

"Five points for grumpy fathers who check out Russian girls in short shorts when their wives aren't looking," he said.

"Two points for everyone who got the Parthenon confused with the Pantheon."

"Four points for duck-lip selfies, plus one bonus point if the selfie is taken with a selfie stick."

"One point for all the tourists who will only experience the Acropolis through their smartphone lens."

When we'd both reached twenty points, Jeff left the bench to roam around. I saw him disappear into the crowd with his damp underwear hanging out of his back pocket. I was content to stay put, lazing alone on the bench, eyes half shut, legs warming in the sun. It was blissful. And temporary. Not ten minutes had passed when I felt an inner alarm bell yanking me out of my catnap. I scanned the crowds. Jeff's Stetson was bobbing low to the ground about fifty feet away. He was crouched behind a marble slab, messing with something in front of the Parthenon. Something was definitely up. I sprang off the bench, made a beeline for the hat, and found him nervously beaming in front of a low wire fence. My mouth dropped. He had converted the wire into a makeshift laundry line. His cherry underwear were drying directly in front of the looming Parthenon entrance.

"What the *hell* are you doing?" I was horrified.

"Perfect. You're just in time," he said, pretending not to notice my shock. "Can you take a picture of me drying my boxers at the Parthenon? We've gotta make it quick. Guards everywhere."

"Jesus, you have no shame," I hissed.

"That's why you like me. Quick. Take it. Hundred points for this one." He shoved his iPhone into my hands. I disapprovingly complied, hoping to avoid a scene. But I wasn't fast enough.

"RESPECT!" A guard waved his two-way radio at us from a nearby thicket of columns. He was moving towards us furiously, his face redder than Jeff's underwear.

"You're paying for bail," I said.

"Laundry's done. Time to go," said Jeff, still grinning nervously. He snatched up his underwear, grabbed my hand, and pulled me into a crowd of elderly French women.

"Pardon mademoiselles! Pancho and Lefty coming through. Trying to outrun the federales!"

. . .

"What's the line between pushing boundaries and being a complete asshat?" I asked as we made our way back down the long cascade of Propylaea steps.

"Are my antics finally too much, baby?" He laughed.

"Come on, Jeff. I'm being serious."

The wattage of his grin dimmed to an appropriate level of gravity. He was in trouble and he knew it. "Okay. Every once in a while I take things too far, but what people don't realize is that I'm constantly assessing risk, I care about the stuff that actually matters, and I've never intentionally caused harm to anyone else. *Ever.*"

"That's true," I agreed. "You're never malicious or manipulative. But you *knew* you were crossing a line."

"Technically I was hanging something *on* a line," he said contritely. "But I may have gotten a little carried away."

"God, you're practically Diogenes reincarnated," I said. "I can picture him drying his underwear in front of the Parthenon with the *exact* same twisted grin on his face."

He gave me a repentant smile. "I love it when a beautiful woman compares me to a dead guy who used to defecate in public."

I gave him a dirty look. Despite his protestations, comparisons were definitely in order. Diogenes the Cynic was a rebel philosopher who had probably torn out of the Acropolis a time or two back in the fourth century B.C. He earned his reputation with bizarre (and often obscene) public stunts intended to critique the prevailing social strictures of his day. Diogenes was all about concrete action over intellectual theory. He lived in a ceramic barrel in the Athenian marketplace to advocate a life of simplicity. He carried a lantern in broad daylight asking where he could find an honest man. He urinated on his enemies, masturbated in public, and, yes, defecated in the theatre as a declaration of his independence from state and society. Even his death was a winking joke—no one knows exactly how he met his end, but the rumours range from holding his own breath to raw octopus poisoning.

As far as comparisons went, Jeff had considerably more polish and charm. He'd never pissed on a testy colleague, tenured or not. On the other hand, he had forsaken most of his worldly possessions to live in a used dumpster, he took a special delight in causing public scenes, and he too lived to provoke the system.

Jeff's obsession with system bending wasn't driven by ulterior motives. He wasn't enticed by money or prestige (though, it must be said—he didn't mind them). If he had any end-goal it was simply to carve out unusual spaces for experimentation within the standard morass of rule and order. He didn't butt up against social norms out of punk-rock rebellion. He pushed back because he felt surprising leaps were most likely to occur in structures with open, fluid environments. Like a boy in a blanket fort, he was drawn to create magical worlds within ordinary ones. Playful disruption was the only thing that held his attention. I imagined him as the joker in a deck of cards. He was the wild card that could be adapted to any role or suit, the trump card that could change the trajectory of a game with a single play. In some games, the joker was the most desirable card. In others, it was the most risky one to draw.

. . .

If Jeff was the joker, I was something far less attention-grabbing. The eight of spades, maybe. I was just as much a rebel, but I would never be caught airing my laundry at the Parthenon. I carried out my insurgencies stealthily, in the shadows. After years of mounting religious doubt I led a quiet coup d'état against the evangelical party line soon after my homeschool graduation. I parsed out the entire history of Christianity dating back to the Council of Nicea and then washed my hands of the whole business with an ambitious manifesto titled "A Treatise on the Boundaries of Religion: Or Why I Am Not A Christian Anymore." I showed the manifesto to no one. Instead, I advanced to the next set of banned books: Darwin's *On the Origin of Species* (the earth wasn't created in six days after all) and J. K. Rowling's *Harry Potter* (filed under the witchcraft category).

In my first year of community college, I walked into my parents' bathroom with a pair of craft scissors and chopped off the long blonde tresses I'd grown out during high school. It was a hack job, but I felt a rush of satisfaction with each metallic snip. The cleavered hair was my subtle coat of arms as I ventured into the taboo realms of premarital sex. I ran my fingers through its short silkiness as I rolled forbidden words off my tongue (*fuck/shit/hell*). When my sociology professor asked who in the room considered themselves a feminist, I was one of two people who raised my hand.

Jeff and I transgressed in different ways, but when we were together, I was the stealthy wallflower caught up in the orbit of our experimental world (one that we *had* created in six days). It was surreal. "You're the first person to make me feel like I'm inside one of my own dreams," I told him in bed a few weeks after we met. In the handful of weeks between meeting on OkCupid and taking off to Istanbul, my newly stable life had been swept into a frenzied tornado. I could hardly catch a breath. But after two years of staring at my bedroom ceiling, I didn't want to. I craved his chaos. I wanted to be baptized in wildness.

I liked the way he could never sit still. I liked the way my hair whipped in my eyes when he barreled us down Texas back roads with Merle Haggard blaring. I liked that I'd seen more of the Lone Star State in the past five weeks than in the last twelve years combined. I liked the way he converted my 2-by-3 cement porch into a margarita bar and spontaneously invited everyone in my apartment complex over for drinks (most of whom I'd never met). I liked the heady sense of possibility that he constantly summoned. Anything could happen at anytime. Any place could be converted into a portal for adventure: gas stations, toiletry aisles, dive bars with sticky floors.

One weekend, on a whim, he invited me to spend the night at *his place*—the University of Texas-Brownsville office that doubled as his illegal squatter home. It was five hours away, but in Texas a five-hour drive is nothing more than a quick pop to the next town over. We left Austin and cruised south through sugarcane fields and the steamy deltas of the Rio Grande Valley.

It's difficult to describe the magic of the Valley, a land that doesn't feel quite like Texas or Mexico though it's suspended between both. On the drive down I imagined Brownsville would resemble its name—a hot, dusty border town similar to El Paso or Laredo—but it's surprisingly lush. A warm subtropical dreamland of palm trees and swamps filled with nesting herons.

Flocks of green parrots sailed overhead as we pulled into campus and parked in an empty student lot a stone's throw from the Mexican border. "Stay close to me," said Jeff, placing his hand on the small of my back. We had to be discreet. The campus was closing down for the night. I felt a teenage thrill as I followed him down a circuitous path that bypassed the security cameras stationed around his building. We were breaking rules. We might be caught.

"I really like what you've done with the place," I said as he swept me out of the empty science hallway and into his office. All four walls were painted blood red, which lent the room a certain opium den allure. The décor was minimal. The giant painting of his suicidal great-great-grandfather looked out over a single stainless steel desk, an office chair, a blackout curtain, and a giant Persian carpet that had once belonged to his mother. That was it.

"You like it?" he joked. "It's going to be on the cover of *Dwell* next month."

Like many a bookish college girl, I'd suffered a handful of professorial crushes during my university career. I never took it farther than overcompensating on my assignments and going to office hours with fake questions about Keynesian economics. All my seduce-the-professor fantasies remained firmly in the realm of fantasy where they belonged. But now, with an eligible professor and a locked office, I was in the rare position to actually follow through on a schoolgirl fantasy. *Sort of.*

"Say 'hello' to my little friend," said Jeff, pointing to the painting of Abner in his lacy baptismal dress. "I think he likes you." A black polyester sleeping bag manifested from out of his recycling bin. He stretched it out on the Persian carpet and motioned to me. *A bed for the lady.* For himself, he pulled out a felted Kazakh rug and set it beside my sleeping bag. For the final touch of romance, he pulled out the lone book in his office—*The Red Book*, Carl Jung's collection of mystical art—and opened it to a painting of a wounded snake with blood gushing out of its severed legs. He laid the painting on the carpet just behind my trout-print camping pillow. "You won't believe the dreams you have with this thing by your head."

After that he set me on top of his cold steel desk and

started kissing down my neck. "Looks like my desk is *just* the right the height for you," he whispered. That was my cue to unbutton my shirt and forget about severed snake limbs and sleeping bags. Reality, for once, was keeping pace with my fantasies. Office sex was hot. It was raunchy and pornographic. Not to mention kinky with his child ancestor watching from the wall. The act was heightened by the risk of security guards, which turned Jeff on. He liked his sex with a side of risk.

A week earlier, he'd smuggled me into a Freudian psychologist's office in broad daylight. We were visiting one of his high school friends in an old house that had been converted into offices. The psychologist had the office next door, but she was out to lunch. Jeff tried the doorknob. It wasn't locked. He pulled me into her Victorian-era quarters and we sat on the fancy chaise lounge, fingering the cushions.

"Tell me about your mother," I said.

"Tell me why you're still in your jeans," he replied, slowly running his hand up my leg to the bronze button above my zipper.

"Jeff, no way. We can't do it on a Freudian chaise lounge."

"Why not? Freud never shut up about sex. I'm pretty sure we have his blessing."

"What if the psychologist comes back and finds us fornicating on her couch?"

"I'll ask if she's willing to go on retainer. Freud knows I could use some help."

For a formerly chaste, homeschooled Christian girl, doing it on a Freudian chaise lounge was curiously liberating. But even the chaise lounge couldn't top the night when Jeff pulled off Interstate 37 between Corpus Christi and San Antonio and parked the car just off the highway access road. The place was abandoned except for a semitruck. Waylon's "I've Always Been Crazy" was coming through the stereo.

"I'll be right back." That was the only information he supplied before leaving the car and wading through the thick mounds of purple threeawn grass between the semi truck and us. I froze as he climbed inside the unlocked cab. This was shotgun country. He knew it as well as I did. Trespassing in Texas could earn you a bullet in the brain or a load of buckshot in the face. I held my breath, waiting for a flurry of expletives and *bam bam* of gunshots.

For the longest time there was nothing, and then, after I was sure a trucker had wrung Jeff's head right off his neck, I saw an arm waving from inside the cab. He wanted me to come—no pun intended. My boots rustled up the scent of ripe grass with each step towards the truck. We were in the middle of nowhere. Nothing but crickets and lonely cars beneath the faint band of the Milky Way. There were worse places to die. As I neared the front tires a hand reached out to pull me inside. The cab was bigger than I expected. It was dark but I could see a rip in the seat. Yellow foam was spilling out. There were empty cans on the floor. It smelled mildewy and stale, like a man who spent too much time alone. Then, before I could notice anything else, Jeff's mouth was heavy on mine.

"I'm too nervous to be turned on," I said between kisses. "How do you know the driver isn't around?"

"Don't worry," he joked. "I'm pretty sure it's abandoned. There's no one here but us . . . and the entire interstate." His hands were searching for my waistband, but they paused when he sensed my stiffness. He drew back and studied me in the dim flashes of southbound headlights. "Hey," he said, quietly. "You're safe with me."

Those four words, the way he said them without any pretense—*you're safe with me.* It was like the briefest suggestion of a figure in an abstract painting, a small bit of definition to anchor the scene. It was the rowdy outlaw briefly setting down his gun. Never mind that the meaning of "safe" was just as undefined as everything else in our boundary-less play-ground. The words were enough to convince me to surrender to the moment, to the dark truck and the swaying purple threeawn grass and my pants on the floor with the empty plastic bottles and Fritos packages. I gave myself to pleasure. It seemed like the thing to do.

CHAPTER 9 | Know Thyself

"Would y'all point us in the direction of the Eiffel Tower?" said Jeff. He said it with a deadpan southern twang, like he had a wad of chewing tobacco tucked in the corner of his mouth. Without waiting for an answer, he unfolded a wadded map of Athens across the car rental counter. "We've already been to the Acropolis, but that damned tower is nowhere to be seen."

The middle-aged rental clerk was flummoxed. He cleared his throat, straightened his jacket, and peered deeply into his computer screen. "Sir, I regret to inform you that the Eiffel Tower is . . . in Paris, which is 2,953 kilometres away. Perhaps you might be interested in a longer rental period?"

"Well, dag nab it," said Jeff. "I coulda sworn it was around here somewhere." He looked at me. "Darlin', will your heart be broke if we save Italy for another trip?"

I rolled my eyes. "Fine with me, honey." He took a special pleasure in channeling geographically challenged Americans, but I was tired and not much in the mood to play along.

The clerk hid an appalled smile in the arm of his jacket and pretended to cough. "Excuse me. Very good, sir. Please follow me." He led us out of the air-conditioned office and into the late afternoon heat, where he handed Jeff a key to a dark silver Citroen hatchback. *Have a nice trip, sir.*

Jeff tipped his hat as I settled into the passenger seat and tugged my seat belt tightly across my chest. "I would give you shit for messing with innocent bystanders, but why bother if we're going to join the great beyond as soon as we pull out of the parking lot?"

Athenian traffic was legendary. Traffic lanes were decorative suggestions, street signs were often obscured (if they were present at all), and fellow drivers often seemed to be reenacting a racing scene from *The Fast and the Furious*.

Jeff knew the facts but was unperturbed. "Don't worry, baby. This is gonna be fun." His eyes lit up as he switched on the ignition, slammed the gearshift in reverse, and rapidly backed the car right to the edge of a congested six-lane artery.

My knuckles were white from gripping the map. "No

offense, but do you actually know what you're doing?"

"Well, darlin', I guess we're about to find out," he said. "Now, which way to Delphi?"

. . .

The ruins of Delphi on the Aegean Coast were the historical home of the Oracle of Delphi. Jeff had mentioned the Oracle to me in one of our initial OkCupid emails. She was a mysterious prophetess whose divine auguries wielded great power in ancient Greece. After studying her history I'd felt strongly drawn to her archetype—and her home, Delphi, a mountain city the ancient Greeks considered the centre of the universe. Jeff felt the same way. We couldn't go so far as to *plan* a side trip out of Athens, but the underwear debacle at the Acropolis was a good enough reason as any to splurge on the cost of a rental car and skip out of town for a night.

I don't remember the actual skipping out of town. My hands flew over my eyes as soon as Jeff pulled out of the rental car parking lot and into the bedlam of traffic. Closing my eyes was a safety precaution. It meant fewer frantic obscenities that could potentially distract from the road. Jeff was a skilled traffic wrangler, but that knowledge did nothing to stop me from hyperventilating every time a motorcyclist revved down a row of gridlocked cars or a taxi driver inched up on our license plate like we were playing bumper cars. (*Shit! Shit! Oh my god!*)

Jeff didn't know I'd been in a nasty car accident in college. The accident was my fault. It involved spilled cranberry juice, a white skirt, and two seconds of distraction. By the time I looked up from the red stain on my lap the car was already in the middle of an airborne triple roll off a highway entrance ramp. It landed with the wheels facing the sky. Hanging upside down, covered in blood-red cranberry juice in a totaled minivan gave me ample opportunity to reflect on the fundamental madness of getting from point A to point B in giant chunks of steel powered by flammable liquid.

Years later, cars still occasionally triggered a spontaneous fight or flight response. My hands shot out to clutch the door handle. I pumped my foot on brakes that weren't there. I bleated like a dying lamb. It was exactly what my mom used to do during our parent-taught drivers ed sessions in the Dodge family van.

Hysteria began to tighten my chest as Jeff wove in and out of traffic. "Oh, my god, Jeff. I'm turning into my mom. And I know it's inevitable to turn into your parents, and my parents are cool, but I'm watching it happen right before my eyes. I mean, obviously it's not happening *right* in front of my eyes because my eyes are closed, but what I'm trying to say is, first I'm pumping invisible brakes and then what? Life insurance policies? Five kids? How much do babysitters even cost these days?"

"*What!* What are you talking about?" His voice was strained. "Can you open your eyes and check the map? I can't drive and translate highway signs at the same time."

"I scream every time I open my eyes."

"Okay . . . ," he said, trying to think. "Don't look out the window. Just look down at the map. Do you see a northbound highway towards a city that's spelled with a *theta*, then . . . um . . . an upside-down wishbone thingy, a *delta* . . ."

I cut him off, my voice raising a pitch higher with every word. "I don't know the Greek alphabet. I wasn't a physics major and I was too weird to join a sorority. I don't even own a goddamn hair straightener!"

"*Jesus christ.* I really need you to look out the window, watch the signs, and try not to scream. I keep thinking I'm about to hit a pedestrian and it turns out to be some guy turning on his left blinker."

"Okay, okay. I'm sorry," I said, trying to contain myself. "I hate to be freaking out like this, but sometimes I just get . . . *anxious*. And I go on about the great beyond and invisible brakes. Do you want to drop me on the side of the road?"

"No way," he muttered. "I told you there's nothing you can do that will scare me and I meant it. Plus, your freakouts are better than HBO."

. . .

Despite my anxiety attack, we did make it out of Athens alive. Jeff pulled into a tiny seaside town on the Gulf of Corinth after a long, circuitous drive through cornfields and empty coastal hills. The sleepy village of Itea didn't seem to have much going on after dark (or really at any time of day, for that matter). We parked the car in front of the only place that showed signs of life—a little convenience shop with the standard lineup of toiletries and chocolate wafers, plus a deli counter with salami, cheese, and a row of bulk olive jars. A gargantuan, red-faced man with bulging eyes sat half-asleep by the cash register. I didn't want to disturb him. Jeff did it instead.

He marched up to the counter and communicated that we needed a place to stay with a hybrid that was part broken English and part Charlie Chaplin mime show. The red-cheeked man uttered a single word that either meant "wait" or "dancing fool." Then he picked up a phone with fingers that looked alarmingly large, like the sausages in his deli case.

We loitered around the doorway, waiting in suspense to see who the man had summoned. Bob appeared before long. He was a tall, graying Dutch man who told us he had a room for rent right across the street. The room was a dive. It was lined with faded beach furniture that looked like it had probably been on sale during the Vietnam War. The towels were threadbare and thin. Tiny, gray smudges dotted the walls. I leaned in. They were mosquitos. The only redeeming amenity was the lush, grapevine-covered patio right on the edge of the sea. All for less than a cheap Motel 6.

"Well, it ain't the Hilton," said Jeff, raising an eyebrow at me. "But it's got charm."

"So, we're not compromising the experiment with a room?" I said hopefully. After a week of sleeping in strangers' living rooms, I desperately wanted a room of my own. I would gladly share Bob's bedroom with a kingdom of mosquitos if it meant that, for one night, I could forgo polite conversation and lines for the communal bathroom.

Jeff thought for a second. "Do you think it's cheating? We parked five feet away from the door without knowing where we were. Seems kind of fortuitous."

"Totally fortuitous," I agreed. "And the room even comes with soap."

We handed Bob some cash. As soon as the door clicked behind him we proceeded to do the sorts of things you can only do when you're alone. We got naked. Underwear, bra, and socks went straight to the bathroom sink with Bob's wafer-thin complimentary soap. We ripped the cobweb gray sheets off the bed and wrapped them around our bodies as make-shift mosquito guards. Then we moved out to the patio and sat wordlessly like pale ghosts, sipping cheap beers from the convenience shop, counting waves that we could hear but not see.

Jeff looked at me. "Hey," he said softly. "I wasn't sure how this was going to turn out, but I'm glad you're here. This trip is better than it would have been if I'd gone alone. You see things that I don't see."

"Coming from Mr. One-man-tent, that means a lot," I said.

"Yeah," he said, clinking my beer can. "I guess it does."

. . .

It was different in the morning. I felt rested for the first time since the sleepless Greek ferry ride, but Jeff was peevish. I'd overslept—and not just by a little. It was high noon by the time we rolled out of Bob's mosquito den and headed towards the slopes of Mount Parnassus where Delphi awaited. Jeff had been planning to do his ruins-at-dawn number. Of all the landmarks that he hoped to see in the first light of morning, Delphi was at the top. And now his chance was gone.

Where I tended to express frustration in sudden incoherent streams of consciousness, Jeff went dead silent, forcing me to interpret his discontent through other cues: the slam of Bob's complimentary coffeepot lid, the vehement thrust of his foot through his pant legs, the short, gruff one-liners (*no, fine, let's go*).

Interpreted as a whole, the gist of his monosyllabic grunts and slams seemed to imply that I was slowing him down. He *never* slept in while traveling alone. If it weren't for my lethargy, he would've been sitting at Delphi, watching the morning sun sweep over the sacred ruins (which raised the question: if he'd missed this sunrise, what else had he missed?). Was he worried that he'd compromised his style by bringing me along? Was he paranoid that one compromise would inevitably slide into others—that I might try to wrangle him into four bulging-at-the-seams suitcases, a reservation at the London Savoy, and a Tiffany engagement ring by the end of the trip?

I'd felt a brief twinge of guilt as I brushed my teeth in front of the scratched bathroom mirror, but it was quickly replaced by indignation. A single compromise did not a Savoy reservation make! I scoured the toothbrush roughly across my molars, and then huffed out of the bathroom towards the kitchenette table where he was moodily checking his phone. "Listen," I yelled. "If you want things to be exactly like they are when you travel alone . . . then you should travel ALONE!"

He raised an eyebrow, but didn't react. It was the beginning of a schism in our do-what-you-want doctrine. Sleeping in was what I truly wanted to do. Waking up at dawn was what he truly wanted to do. Neither desire was wrong, but it was impossible to do both. So what then? For all our bohemian aspirations we were still faced with Compromise 101, just like everyone else.

The winding drive up the mountain was silent—and not the easy, comfortable kind. Any peacemaking attempts on my part were met with a grumpy, "I'm fine," though it was obvious he was still morose. In his mind, Delphi would be overrun with tourists and devoid of magic by this hour. But the fear was unfounded. The July sun was broiling Mount Parnassus. The Delphi parking lot was nearly empty and no one appeared to be venturing up the hillside path that led to the fallen Temple of Apollo.

Jeff and I split up as soon we walked through the visitor centre entrance. He headed towards the museum. I pulled my scarf veil-like over my head and began to mount the hill alone. Despite the blistering heat, there was a sacred air that not even our awkward non-fight could dampen. The whole reason we'd made this detour was to visit the Temple of Apollo, where, for over ten centuries, the Oracle of Delphi had delivered divine prophecies in fits of raving madness.

For the ancient Greeks, the rural mountain village of Delphi, surrounded by soaring crags, was the centre of the universe. It seemed fitting somehow that the epicentre was located not at the Parthenon, but on a remote mountain spine overlooking an empty valley punctuated with rugged pine trees and tall, spindly beeches. According to Greek legend, Zeus released two eagles into the sky—one to the east and the other to the west. Their flight paths crossed above Delphi on the slopes of Mount Parnassus, and Zeus promptly declared the backwoods, goat-herding village to be the centre of the world.

Delphi did indeed become the most sacred site of the ancient Greek world. For nearly ten centuries, political rulers, military commanders, and philosophers made pilgrimages from far and wide to consult the Oracle of Delphi's mystic wisdom. In a restrictive era when, as the historian Thucydides tidily summed it up, "the greatest glory for women is to be least talked about among men, whether in praise or blame," the Oracle was a powerful and authoritative female icon.

And it wasn't just one woman, but many. When the presiding Oracle died, the next priestess was selected from the nearby village of Delphi—typically an upstanding older woman with few remaining obligations to children and husband. Upon accepting the position, the Oracle was required to be set apart, to shed all connection with her former identity and focus solely on her role as prophetess. When called on for advice, she descended to a lower level beneath the Temple of Apollo, where she sat on a tripod positioned above a vent in the earth. Steamy vapors rising from the vent sent her into an ecstatic state of union with Apollo, the god of prophecy. It was a sensual business, being entered by god—full of feverish delirium, heaving chests, and revelatory visions.

If Diogenes was Jeff's patron saint, the Oracle of Delphi was mine (Diogenes was actually rumored to have visited the Oracle, who advised him to "deface the currency"). She was an ordinary woman who lived on a remote mountain cliff and channeled the divine by getting high on deep vents in the earth. What wasn't to love?

I sat cross-legged under an olive tree close to the Temple of Apollo, which was now little more than a giant stone slab and a few scraggly pillars. A group of American high school students was also beginning to congregate under the shade of my olive tree—most of them playing the cool disinterest card. No one was paying attention to the tour guide, a regal forty-year-old American woman dressed head-to-toe in white linen.

"Here we are next to the site of the Temple of Apollo where the Oracle used to enter her ecstatic states," she said, projecting her voice across the cluster of languid faces. "Most of the pillars are gone now, but we can imagine how magnificent the temple truly was. We also have to imagine the phrase that was famously engraved across the entrance. It said *gnothi seauton,* which translates to "know thyself". Every person who came to consult the Oracle would have passed beneath those two words—it was her way of warning pilgrims that even the most divine prophecy was useless to someone who had yet to master the self.

Know thyself. I occasionally wonder if every bit of my two-year mental joyride could be boiled down to that one phrase. All the madness, the helpless floundering, the failed starts—all of it just to look in the mirror and truly see what was looking back at me.

Austin was one of my failed starts. Or at least that's how it seemed at the time. After six months of lethargic unemployment at my parents' house in Fort Worth, I moved three hours south to be with my on-again-off-again boyfriend who was studying at the University of Texas at Austin. I hugged my parents goodbye on a cold January morning just after New Year's. Leaving was supposed to be a healthy step towards recovery, but I wept the entire stretch of Interstate 35 between Fort Worth and Austin. I was terrified of being left alone with myself.

Between my mother's patient support and a weekly therapist appointment, I'd stabilized some since the summer. I could force myself to eat, even when my stomach didn't want food (though my diet was mostly limited to peanut-butter-jelly sandwiches, mashed potatoes, and protein shakes); I could enter public spaces—grocery stores, banks, and gas stations—without showing visible signs of anxiety; and I could cover the dark crescents under my eyes with concealer, but those were just coping mechanisms. I still felt like I'd been locked in a room with a maniac and the maniac was me.

Switching cities wasn't a cure. Like a loyal dog, the crazy followed wherever I went, and I went a lot of places. I moved four times in the first six months. First, with my boyfriend, to a yellowing, cinderblock complex near campus. It was called *Villa Arcos*. The swimming pool was filled in with overgrown grass and a palm tree. It didn't resemble a villa in the slightest. My boyfriend did his best to support me in my shaky mental state (he frequently came home to find me immobilized in bed), but the relationship was understandably strained. We didn't survive past March.

Three months after moving to Austin, I found myself newly stranded in a city I hardly knew, frantically trawling Craigslist for cheap rooms to rent. An older guy emailed me and said he had a spare room in a decrepit-but-cool stone mansion on a couple of private acres. There were bats in the kitchen and I had to solemnly swear I would *never, ever* let guests on the property, but rent was cheap and I was desperate. I said yes. After a month he casually offered me drugs and confessed he had plans to turn the place into a nudist colony. I had nothing personal against drugs or nudists, but if no one else was allowed on the property, the nudist "colony" would probably just be him and me, an idea I didn't particularly relish.

I left the burgeoning nudist colony for a one-room cabin south of town. The cabin belonged to a new boyfriend, who I'd met at my weekly warehouse dance. He'd been raised by hippies in a converted school bus out in the Hill Country, which wasn't a problem except for the fact that he wasn't accustomed to turning on the air-conditioning unit in June. I had a sweaty panic attack in a cloud of mosquitos and concluded I wasn't cut out for roommates of any sort. That's when I signed the lease on my little hamster cage efficiency—380 square feet of pure, air-conditioned silence in old West Austin. It was just my demons and me.

I paid for the hamster cage with the part-time admin job I'd finally nailed down after firing out forty résumés a week for three months. The position was with a national therapist association, which seemed just twisted enough to be funny. *A lunatic in the ranks!* Counting me, there were seven employees. They gave me a spacious office, all my own, with a desk-to-ceiling window that overlooked a nature preserve. As long as I answered the phone and filed papers, no one even seemed to notice I was there.

The quiet is what I remember most from my first year in Austin, like a thick blanket of snow had settled over everything. My hamster cage was hushed. The commute to work was muted. My office was a vacuum of soft clicking keys and muffled phone calls. It was like I'd entered purgatory, a foggy gray place where I was neither dead nor alive, but floating somewhere in between, and upside down.

In my office, when I wasn't answering the phone, I spent hours querying Google like it was a fortune teller. (*What is the point of life? Signs that I'm going crazy. How to survive a dark night of the soul.*) I regularly scrolled through anxiety forums where members posted long strings of medication history like they were battle medallions on a jacket: Battle at Atarax, The Last Stand at Lexapro, Klonopin Massacre, Valium War II, and Operation Cymbalta. When my boss walked by, I furtively hid the tabs and cleared my search history, only to crank right back up as soon as she left the hallway.

After over a year of utter dysfunction, I was still under the assumption that I'd lost the "one true path" and would rediscover it only when I identified the correct combination of self-help manuals, Chinese herbal remedies, positive affirmations, and Buddhist mantras. I would rediscover the path only after I'd cleared all my blocked chakras and cataloged all childhood traumas (including the asshole neighbor kid who told me I had donkey teeth when I was ten). Pleiades had to align with Venus. Jesus had to descend from the clouds with a posse of angels. Only then would I find my way.

But if the Oracle's mandate was to *know thyself*, I'd never left the path in the first place. To know myself was not just to know the sunny, sparkly bits but *all* the parts: shadowy corners gathering dust, private fears, old wounds clumsily bandaged but never treated. These sorts of wounds don't fade over time. Pain is patient. Ignoring it in no way makes it gone. It still inhabits the crevices of the body. It settles into the marrow and bone, inventing new ways to push to the surface and make itself known. The longer it's ignored, the more violently creative it gets.

I would've paid no attention to meeting my shadows if my panic hadn't been quite as severe, if the sense of failure hadn't been quite as profound, if I hadn't fallen quite so far down the rabbit hole. The scale of destruction was perfectly calibrated to wake me up. It was an inner Mayday. A grisly right hook to my own face. *You there! Time to pay attention!*

Psychological pain is not an enemy to be tamped down and boxed away. It's a critical warning sensation meant to alert us to the parts of ourselves that need softness and tending. It can be a guide, too, a propelling device that thrusts us, kicking and screaming, down the strange roads most conducive to self-knowledge. Suffering isn't the only route to understanding, but it can be an effective one. Greek pilgrims didn't seek the answers to their deepest questions in the luxury of Athens. They traveled a long and arduous journey to the remote mountain village of Delphi—where the far edge of the world was actually its centre.

. . .

I hadn't moved from beneath the olive tree when Jeff hiked past me, his face flushed from the steep path. We were no more than five feet apart, but he didn't see me. I was so utterly still that I'd become another fixture among the boulders and the burnt, mustard-coloured grass. I whistled softly as he rounded the path leading up to the temple foundation. He froze and turned around, scanning the hillside. Finally, his eyes landed on me.

"You still mad?" I yelled. The words echoed out across the empty valley.

He walked back towards me, hands in his pockets. "Nah," he said sheepishly. "I'm over it. I know better than to have exact expectations of how things should go. We made it to the Oracle. You got some rest. That's what matters."

"Good," I said. "Now, I've got an idea." Together, we migrated away from the olive tree and up to the Temple of Apollo. "This is a little weird, but I think we should ask the Oracle a question," I said.

Jeff's eyes lit up. "Oh yeah—she's definitely still hanging around. Let's write our questions down." We sat down on a carved boulder and pulled out our notebooks. The heat from the stone emanated up through the fabric of my dress, burning my hamstrings. It was quiet except for the low hum of cicadas and the scratch of pencils across page. When we finished our questions, Jeff shielded his page from my view.

"What? Is this like a birthday wish where if you say it out loud it doesn't come true?" I teased. But honestly, I didn't want him to read my question to the Oracle either. It was a private inquiry between her and me: *how do I prepare for where the path leads next?*

CHAPTER 10 | The Long Bus

After the mountain stillness of Delphi, there was nothing I could do to prepare myself for the grueling surrealism of a twenty-three-hour bus trip out of Athens. Sure, I brought a bag of fresh fruit to balance out the greasy rest-stop pastries that threatened my stomach with a two-day intestinal hangover. I attempted to convince my lower spine that my cramped sliver of seat space was some distant relation to the modern bed. I combed my crumpled hair and dabbed on a bit of ChapStick during the quick, ten-minute smoke breaks when all the passengers sleepily filed off the bus and converted the parking lot into a billowing factory, each head a cigarette smokestack.

But, despite my efforts, nothing could prevent the hours from bleeding together like crayons under a hot hairdryer. At some point—after X number of border crossings, Y number of gas stations, and Z number of numb appendages—I began to lose track of which country I was passing through. A few sleepless hours later, in the dead of night, I began to forget where it was I even intended to go in the first place. I forgot my entire life before the bus. The endless sequence of streetlights and empty fields temporarily hypnotized me into believing that the bus was all there is and all there has ever been.

Or at least that's how I felt when we finally made it to Budapest.

. . .

We never planned to go so far north. Jeff's cutout map of Turkey and the Balkans only went as far as Serbia. But Serbia wasn't on the table. We checked before we left Athens for Delphi. "All buses to Belgrade full," the travel agent announced firmly. She had blonde highlights and no-nonsense fuchsia nails that clicked across her keyboard.

"No problem," said Jeff. "Where else can we go?"

"Where else do you *want* to go?" asked the agent.

"You can choose," he said. "We don't care."

The agent raised a skeptical, finely groomed eyebrow at both of us and then pointed towards a large map on the wall. "You choose."

Jeff turned to me. "Where to? You wanna make the call on this one?"

It was my turn to decide. I hesitantly walked to the map and ran my index finger along the different routes. *Krakow. Novi Sad. Budapest. Which one?* It was easy making decisions for myself, but I'd rather lasso feral tomcats than make decisions for other people. I was afraid of the responsibility—afraid that I'd choose something that everyone else secretly hated or that every aggravation occurring from that point onwards (flat tires, stolen passports, receding polar ice caps) would somehow be traced back and blamed on my single, less-than-stellar decision. When it came to minor group decisions, passive flexibility was the safest route to avoiding potential conflict and its fury of attending emotions. It was a protective mechanism.

But my hesitancy also confused me. I wasn't living up to my imaginary Rosie the Riveter ideal. Rosie had formidable biceps and a stare that could melt steel. She knew what she wanted. She wasn't afraid to assert herself. Was I failing Feminism 101 by not having clearly articulated opinions and desires? Was I weak for wanting someone else to choose the next dot on the map? What was so hard about picking a city?

I swung my finger ten latitudes to the north, just to prove that I could. "Let's go to Budapest," I said decisively. "I've always wanted to see the Danube." The firmness in my voice surprised me. I started to backtrack. "I mean, that is if *you* want to see the Danube. I could always do Macedonia, too. Or even..."

"There's no wrong answer!" said Jeff. "Two tickets to Budapest, please."

"It's a twenty-three-hour trip," said the agent, clicking her hibiscus-pink nails. "Bus leaves Thursday at 6 a.m. Don't be late."

. . .

On a cross-country bus, entertainment is limited to staring out the window, playing solitaire until your phone dies, and psychoanalyzing everyone else on the bus. In the people-watching department, my options were limited to the snoring elderly couple sitting across from us and the bus driver, a balding man who sat in front of a placard that read "No Smoking" while holding the steering wheel in his right hand and a lit cigarette in his left. All other voyeurism was limited to rest stops and border crossings.

I spotted Laser Eyes, a fellow passenger, when we

stopped for Macedonian passport stamps. "Six o'clock. We've got an alien sighting at six o'clock. Roger. Niner, niner," I whispered into Jeff's ear.

Jeff casually turned his head to the six o'clock position and then whipped it back around. "Oh my God, he's really half-assed his human disguise."

"Alien" was our code word for people who didn't seem like they were quite of this world—in this case, a guy who looked like he was fresh off the spacecraft. He wasn't tall, but he was built like a tank with meaty, bolt-on biceps and a slicked back mullet that fell just above his hulking shoulders. He was probably forty. Ambiguous ethnicity. Levi's jeans. It was his eyes that were the real giveaway—they were ice-blue lasers that cut into everything they touched.

I brushed past him as we walked back to the bus, stamped passports in hand. He was just standing in line, coolly smoking as his eyes carved fissures into my being.

"Holy shit. He's looking at me," I said under my breath.

"No, I'm pretty sure he was looking at *me*," said Jeff.

"You know what? It's almost like he's looking in every direction at once, like a mutant Mona Lisa."

"Panoptical powers. Good one," said Jeff

"I think he's a sadistic hitman," I whispered as we took

our seats. "Like instead of just taking you out in a dark alley with a silencer, he telepathically intuits your darkest phobia and builds an elaborate death trap. Maybe you open your closet in the morning and instead of J. Crew it's filled with venomous spiders."

"Could be," said Jeff. "Or maybe he's a ghost who has been sentenced to an eternity of riding the bus from Athens to Budapest and back."

Jeff and I could turn anything into a game. We were like kids with a cardboard refrigerator box. In any other hands, the box was a mundane piece of recycling, but in our hands it was a shimmering time machine or a deep-sea submersible. Back in Austin we'd invented all sorts of games. Sometimes we'd stake out a café or a coffee shop. I'd go in first, order something, and sit down. Then he'd come in, order something, and sit down at the table next to mine. We'd pretend to be strangers. Then, gradually, the scene would escalate.

He'd loudly ask if I could pass the salt. I'd ask if he was a Pisces. He'd inquire as to which 'NSYNC member was my favorite ("*Joey, obviously*"). I'd swear I saw him on Tinder ("*Wasn't that you? Holding a trout with your shirt off?*"). He'd swear that he'd invented Facebook while Mark Zuckerberg was still in diapers. I'd confide that I grew up in the Amazon because my parents were Jehovah's Witness missionaries. By the end of lunch, he'd be reaching over to my table to steal bites of eggs Benedict off my plate. I'd be jotting down my number in his notebook. (*"But don't call me before 10 p.m. because that's when my shift at Adult Video ends. I can totally get you five percent off if you're interested."*) Shock and awe complete, we'd fly out of the restaurant, leaving a crowd of dropped jaws in our wake.

Jeff played with his daughter the same way he played with me. On his weekends, they rambled through different cities—College Station, Houston, San Antonio, and Austin—digging treasures out of dumpsters, painting chalk unicorns in Kroger parking lots, looking for dragons in musty street grates. In Sibel's mind, the thought of her father moving into a used dumpster was a perfectly acceptable proposition. Daddy's new house was a fort! A secret cave! The ultimate hide-and-seek spot! As a five-year-old, she possessed his same fearless, easygoing nature. Everything was a game.

And it was true for me, too—everything from Macedonian parking lots to dumpsters could be fantastic if observed through a certain lens, one that acknowledged the mere fact of *being* as a tremendously strange event given our location on the outer arm of the Milky Way galaxy in a 14-billion-year-old universe speckled with 100 billion other galaxies. Jeff and I were both of the opinion that since we'd won two genetic tickets to this earth lottery we were going to play and play hard, goddammit. We were going to take off with no baggage. We were going to jump on the twenty-three-hour bus to Budapest.

. . .

I checked for Laser Eyes when the bus finally deposited us in a vacant Budapest bus station, but if he was there we couldn't see him, which was fine by me. The last thing I wanted was to be stared at by a ghost. It was 5 a.m. and Jeff and I had both reached critical filth levels. The filth had nothing to do with lack of baggage—I would have smelled like something left in the refrigerator too long even if I'd brought along a field of lavender and a five-piece luggage set. There was simply no getting around the hygienic perils of such a long ride.

We had a Couchsurfing host arranged, but the sun hadn't even begun to rise and it was too early to knock on her door and beg for a shower. With nothing else to do, we took an underground tram to the central district and began sleepily drifting down empty streets.

It's rare to first meet a city in its flinty, pre-dawn stillness—you end up interpreting the city by its façades instead of by its faces. The façades of Budapest were a mystery. They reminded me of other European cities I'd seen—almost like the buildings had been plucked from Paris, Vienna, and Berlin and then set back down along the banks of the Danube in a pastiche of Art Nouveau embellishments, Baroque domes, and Gothic arches.

Buda Castle, the Baroque hilltop palace visible from almost any point in Budapest, is a fossil record of Hungary's tumultuous fortune—its lofty walls have been besieged more than thirty-one times. The Tatars came through, as did the Turks and the Habsburgs. Half a million Hungarian Jews were killed under German occupation during the Holocaust, and in 1956 the Soviets rolled in squadrons of tanks to squelch the Hungarian revolution against the Warsaw Pact (forcing Hungary to remain in the Eastern Bloc until the 1990s).

Yet despite centuries of tumult, a powerful Hungarian ethos survived and resurged. The Magyar undercurrent is preserved in the language itself—a songlike tongue that bears almost no relation to any other European language, despite Hungary being set smack-dab in the middle of the continent.

It's in the Hungarian cuisine, with strong flavors of paprika, pepper, saffron, and ginger. It's the character of a people who combine hot-blooded courage and merry hospitality with melancholy and national sadness. *"Sírva vigad a Magyar,"* goes the old saying. Hungarians cry while having fun.

. . .

According to her Couchsurfing profile, Dorottya was a late-twenties film critic. *Writer, dreamer, hitchhiker.* She had pale freckles and flaming red hair tied up in a loose ponytail. She immediately struck me as the kind of person whose soft-spoken exterior hid an inner wildness. "I'm behind on a film review. Hope you don't mind fending for yourself," she told us during the cursory tour of the homey, wood-paneled flat she shared with three other roommates. She opened a tall, wooden door into a sunlit room decorated with a patchwork of college-student furniture. "My roommate is out of town," she said. "You can stay here."

I almost kissed her feet when she told us we could shower and toss our clothes in the washing machine. "But if you *really* want to feel clean, you should try one of the Hungarian bathhouses," she said. "There are over a hundred thermal springs in Budapest."

"Thanks, but I avoid anything related to soap or water unless absolutely necessary," said Jeff, which was no exaggeration (he reserved a specific facial expression for his once-weekly shower, a pained grimace, like a little boy with soap in his eyes).

Unlike Jeff, I was of the Sylvia Plath school of thought when it came to bathing. *I never feel so much myself as when I'm in a hot bath*, she wrote. And I agreed. To me, baths were safe houses—womblike sanctuaries where nothing and no one could intrude (not even smartphones). If I weren't concerned with depleting the aquifers, I would happily sit under a shower head until my entire body morphed into a pale, wrinkly prune. My parents could confirm that. Before I moved out (the first time) they used to bang on the bathroom door, reminding me that out of all five kids I was the one singlehandedly jacking up their water bill. *I can't help it,* I wanted to yell through the door. *This is where I feel safe.*

They say water represents emotion in dreams. Churning oceans. Placid lakes. Swollen rivers. I certainly had enough of that to go around. It had taken me most of my life to realize that my nervous system was more sensitive than the average kid on the block. Not everyone walked into a party and intuitively felt the inner emotional landscape of the guy doing Jell-O shots.

As a kid, I could gauge my mother's morning mood by the weight of her step on the staircase. When my dad turned on *The Karate Kid,* I could viscerally feel the sick crunch when Johnny, the bully, delivers an illegal blow to Daniel's knee in the final fight scene. The boundaries between the outside world and myself were porous and paper-thin. I was constantly awash in emotion—some of it my own, but much of it not. The bathtub was my escape—the one hiding place where everything washed off my body and down the dark, swirling slot of the drain.

. . .

Dorottya recommended I baptize myself in the thermal baths at Hotel Gellert, a famous and longstanding Budapest icon on the western bank of the Danube—the Buda side. Before a relatively recent municipal marriage in 1873, the city of Budapest was actually two cities—the rolling, castle-graced hills of Buda to the west; the bustling, bourgeois plains of Pest to the east; and the misty gray ribbon of the Danube splitting down the middle (or *Duna*, as the locals call it). Both sides of the city were easy to navigate. A brief rickety tram ride across the river delivered me right to the front steps of the Hotel Gellert, an imperial Art Nouveau gem right on the water.

An unexpected wave of intimidation washed over me as I strolled into the century-old grand entry hall in my grimy dress. The lobby featured a two-story vaulted glass cupola, ornate pillars, and a bevy of naked statues set inside red velvet wall recesses. It was more like an old world palace than a spa. The whole building was a living memorial to the days when telegraphs and tobacco pipes were all the rage. The effect was so convincing I half considered giving a small, ceremonial curtsy to the attendant who handed me a swimsuit and pointed me in the direction of the locker rooms.

On the way to the lockers, I mulled over whether or not there was a Hungarian bathing code. *If so, what was it? Were swimming caps mandatory? Would anyone take offense to the ungroomed jungle between my legs?* Ironically, it was my pre-occupation with committing a cultural faux pas that led me to commit one. I walked into the dressing room only to find myself surrounded by hairy bellies and dangling man bits. I was standing in a phallus forest. I'd never seen so many in one place—except maybe in *National Geographic* or the black-and-white photos of my mother's copy of *The Family of Man.* The only words I could manage were, "Oh dear."

Fortunately, my navigational error was quickly corrected. *This way, madam. A* male attendant politely steered me away from the man bits and towards the women's locker room. My cheeks were still burning by the time I put on my rented navy Speedo and walked out to the complex of pools, though the embarrassment was somewhat mitigated by the realization that I'd entered some sort of bathing nirvana. There were enough pools for a Dr. Seuss poem: indoor pools, outdoor pools, hot pools, cold pools, mineral pools, and wave pools.

I made my way towards the wave pool, carefully avoiding eye contact with any man whose leg-hair looked familiar. Thankfully, the gentle undulations of the pool lulled away the memory of dangling genitalia and sketchy bus stop bathrooms. This was the rhythm of travel—exhausting marathons of movement punctuated by surprising moments of calm where time slowed and there was nowhere to be except right here, floating, eyes closed.

The liquid calm lasted an hour at the most. I'm not sure exactly when the coal-coloured clouds began to gather, but I know I wasn't the only one pretending not to notice the dark wall that had migrated from the distant horizon to a position directly above the Hotel Gellert wave pool. Our collective denial came to an abrupt end with the first timpani crash of thunder. I'd seen enough Texas summer storms to know that this was going to be a real tempest. The wind picked up, whipping over signs and pool chairs. The wave pool suddenly stopped waving as a few fat drops of rain split open on the sunbathing terrace. Kids screamed as rain began to pelt the deck in earnest. Parents were screaming too as they rushed to gather flip-flops and swim towels.

I left the wave pool and stood outside the locker rooms where women were shrieking through the entrance. There was something delightful about having an excuse to open up the lungs for a nice, long scream. Besides football games and concerts, there aren't many opportunities for public displays of volume—screaming, shrieking, and howling. Which is a shame, because there's something odd and deeply satisfying about belting out from the bottom of your gut every now and then. I screamed, too, in my rented Speedo out in the torrential downpour, the lone bather on the empty Hotel Gellert pool deck. And it felt good, like water always does.

. . .

The Hotel Gellert was not my first public demonstration of emotion. I gave an equally rousing performance during the second summer of crazy. It was on a different sort of day—the kind of sweltering Texas afternoon when the cicadas screech from the trees like the apocalypse is nigh. My parents were in Austin visiting for the weekend and I'd taken them to an art exhibit on the University of Texas campus.

I don't remember a single stroke of paint from the exhibit. All I remember is afterwards: the bright-eyed college students confidently striding across campus with backpacks full of textbooks and futures full of plans. My father, the architect, was snapping photos of rounded cornices, but I was honing in on the backpacks. Backpacks, like briefcases, were a type of baggage that conveyed purpose. Even if it was an illusion, the backpacked students had purpose. They were probably going to be lawyers, doctors, and marketing directors. At dinner parties, they would have self-assured answers when confronted with the inevitable question of, "So, what do *you* do?" over martinis.

I craved their certainty. But it was so far out of reach. I'd been rotating a mental Rubik's Cube for a year and a half and was still no closer to cracking the algorithm than when I'd started.

As I stood under the shadow of the University of Texas clock tower, it occurred to me that I had no guarantee my searching would eventually culminate in some grand revelation or recovery. Maybe I'd never solve for X. Maybe I'd never be certain the universe was anything more than a cold, chaotic space littered with stars, ad infinitum. Maybe I'd never comprehend the randomness with which pain, suffering, and death so often seemed to strike. Maybe I'd never be able to shake my madness. Maybe I'd never find my way back to normal.

The sidewalk epiphany was more than a case of sheltered white girl from the suburbs realizing that not even her privilege could save her from suffering and uncertainty (though, admittedly, there was that). The heaviness encompassed me, but it also extended far beyond.

All of us were caught up in a mad, mad world that no one seemed totally sure how to reckon with. Religion offered comfort, obviously, but what if you weren't completely sold on an invisible spirit in the sky? What then? ("You're on Earth. There's no cure for that," wrote Samuel Beckett.)

Uncertainty gathered in my chest as I walked beside my parents. Then, without warning, a guttural howl rose in my throat and swooped out of my mouth. Tears hit the sidewalk.

By the time I realized they were my own it was already too late. I was over the edge, publicly weeping for anyone who cared to watch.

My parents made no attempt to hush me. They didn't even ask what was wrong. They simply wrapped their arms around me and held me tight. It was the only firm answer they themselves could give.

CHAPTER 11 | The Road to Sarajevo

I felt a shiver when the word "hitchhiking" came out of Dorottya's mouth. It was our second night in Budapest and she was in the kitchen, chopping carrots and adding them to a pot of Hungarian *goulash* that had already been simmering for hours. Jeff and I were sitting at the table poring over a map of the Balkans after a day of relaxed wandering across the city.

"You know, if you really want to test the unknown, you should try hitchhiking to Sarajevo," said Dorottya. "It's the best feeling in the world. You have no idea who's going to come down the road or when you're going to get your next ride. Anything can happen."

I studied the tangle of roads on the map, considering her suggestion. At a purely analytical level, I was opposed to the idea of handing our fate to the whims of the road.

Hitchhiking was safer and more common in Europe than in the United States, but even with our nomadic approach there were still too many uncontrolled variables for my comfort. In two days we were scheduled to fly from southern Croatia to the United Kingdom for the third and final leg of our trip. That meant we had five hundred miles and two border crossings between our next milestone and us. We were running out of time for surprises.

On the other hand, there was the shiver—the subtle inner draw, like someone had wrapped a cord of rope around my waist and was gently, but firmly, tugging me down a different, more interesting path. Hitchhiking was not our brightest idea, but I had a feeling that, one way or another, we were going to end up on a road with our thumbs out.

Jeff chimed in. "We haven't bought bus tickets. I don't even think we have much of a choice."

I briefly meditated on the image of us stranded on a Bosnian highway and then brushed it aside. "What the hell. Let's do it," I said. "We'll wake up early and hitchhike to Sarajevo."

"Yes!" said Jeff.

"Don't worry. It's actually very easy," said Dorottya, as she stirred the steaming, paprika-scented pot. "Especially for women. Drivers are more comfortable picking up a woman. All you do is stick out your thumb, make eye contact, and wait. When someone stops to offer you a ride, you look into their eyes and go with your gut instinct. If anything feels strange you can just pass, but it's rare. I've never felt unsafe on any of my rides and I've hitchhiked all over Europe by myself."

"By yourself?" I was in awe. The freckled Dorottya was slender, soft-spoken, and completely devoid of the tough, don't-mess-with-me vibe I assumed was a prerequisite for any woman hitching solo. But maybe my imagination was limited. The idea of women traveling alone was surrounded by false assumptions and an aura of danger—maybe hitchhiking was the same way.

Besides Dorottya, my only other firsthand hitchhiking accounts were from my mother. When she left home on her eighteenth birthday, she headed from San Francisco to Vancouver, Canada, where she celebrated her passage into adulthood by crashing at a cheap hostel. At the hostel she befriended a fellow teenage itinerant who passed on the art of hitchhiking. My restless mother then thumbed her way up the Canadian coast in what was to be the first of many hitchhiking trips across the continent.

The inaugural trip went relatively smoothly—minus the truck driver who rounded the curvy, coastal roads at ninety miles per hour and the seedy, cigar-smoking guy who offered her a job as a "dancer." She spent the first night alone on a frigid Canadian beach where she slept buried under the sand to preserve her body heat. In her rush to escape San Francisco, she hadn't even packed a sleeping bag in her small rucksack. My mother still shakes her head when she tells the story. "I was so naïve. It's a wonder I didn't end up dead."

Maybe she was naïve, but, like Dorottya, she had a surprising gutsy streak. When I was in high school, she nervously traveled alone to the Middle East—her first overseas trip—to be with my older sister Anna who was about to give birth in Muscat, Oman. During the trip she toured the Sultan Quaboos Grand Mosque, where she discussed the tenets of Islam with a soft-spoken imam. My mother felt a shock of recognition as she listened. The church had taught her that all Muslims were deceived and bound for hell, but there, right in front of her, was the same devotion, the same passion for prayer, the same sense of moral duty and the same claims on absolute truth. The doctrine was slightly different but the fervor was identical. The realization shook her to the bone. She flew back to Fort Worth—back to us—with more questions than answers. It was my mother's inner draw that sparked my family's exodus out of the evangelical church.

. . .

The only catch with the inner draw is that though you can almost always trust it, you can never guarantee that its methodologies will be particularly straightforward. Sometimes you get the magical gut intuitions that result in the planets aligning, and a red velvet carpet unfolding at your feet, and a hot FedEx guy delivering a lifetime supply of Nutella to your front door, but the inner guide is just as liable to lead you out onto the cliff edge, leaving you to fumble around, oblivious to the backwards fact that floundering on the edge is often the very thing that summons the magic.

I didn't expect a red velvet carpet when we tiptoed out of Dorottya's flat early the next morning, but I also didn't expect a major round of fumbling. There were no signs that we were being led to the edge. It was Sunday and the Budapest streets were quiet with the kind of hung-over hush that always fills the streets after late weekend nights. The public trashcans were overflowing with glass beer bottles and cheap takeout wrappers. Jeff plunged arm-deep into one and rustled around like a raccoon, emerging with a couple of musty cardboard panels and a pleased look on his face. We sat on the vacant sidewalk and inked "SARAJEVO" in thick block letters with the red marker Dorottya had given us as a parting gift.

It was going to be a long trek. Sarajevo was 375 miles to the south. To reach it we had to cross the southern Hungarian border, hop across a northern chunk of Croatia, and then cruise south through half of central Bosnia-Herzegovina to finally reach Sarajevo (where we had no place to stay). Coming from the 773-mile-wide state of Texas, 375 miles sounded like a quick half-day jaunt. But we were on hitchhiking time and it was anyone's guess how long that would take.

Armed with a cardboard sign, a bottle of orange juice, and a couple of Hungarian pastries, we set out to seek our fortune at Dorottya's favorite outbound hitchhiking spot. She circled it on our map—a highway entrance ramp on the southern edge of town. To get there we had to take a rickety tram to the part of the city where gloomy Soviet apartment blocs gave way to grassy, overgrown lots and industrial warehouses. That's when the awkward fumbling began.

I'm not quite sure how we got turned around. Maybe it was the fact that our ears couldn't connect the Hungarian street spellings on the map with the words coming out of the tram conductor's mouth. Or maybe we just failed to pay attention. Either way, we tumbled out onto an unknown boulevard, totally disoriented. Jeff stopped random pedestrians for directions, but the only Hungarian words we'd really mastered were "hello" (*sziasztok*) and "goulash."

What followed was a navigational scavenger hunt. A skinny high-school couple told us to get back on the tram. We obeyed, only to have a woman on the tram inform us that, no, we were still heading the wrong direction. Jeff's blood pressure began to rise as we got back off the tram and headed back the way we'd just come. I had to sprint to keep up with his long, frustrated strides. He didn't mind being lost when he *chose* to be lost, but this was different. We had somewhere to be and he was failing to get us there.

At first, I found his disorientation intriguing. Jeff rarely lost his cool. I was conscious that we were losing time in a blur of empty lots and graffitied overpasses, but I was also content to observe his process. But my go-with-the-flow attitude began to dwindle when we ended up in an abandoned train yard after failing to correctly interpret the directions of a neighbour woman who took a garden hoe and generously carved out a map in the mud of her front yard.

"Fuck it!" said Jeff.

"Look, let's forget about Dorottya's lucky hitchhiking spot and just find the nearest highway," I said.

It was getting hot. Beads of sweat were streaming down my legs. A dark liquid band was leaking through the crown of Jeff's Stetson. My throat was dry. The orange juice bottle was already empty and most of the bread was gone. We'd wasted half the morning wandering around the outer sticks of Budapest and I was starting to feel irritable.

My mood took another dive when I noticed my underwear was unusually damp. We stopped at a highway gas station where I confirmed that yes, my period had started and yes, one of my three pairs of underwear was ruined, and yes, I had packed exactly two tampons to last a full day of hitchhiking, plus the last leg of the experiment. I'd checked the calendar before we left, knowing that at some point on the trip I'd have to hunt for additional tampons—I just hadn't expected that point to be while hitchhiking through the Balkans.

I broke the news to Jeff under the shade of the gas station canopy where he was waiting. "Hey, you know yesterday when I ate that entire bowl of chocolate ice cream?"

"Yeah. What about it?"

"It wasn't such a freak event, if you know what I mean."

He thought for a moment and then his eyes got wide. "Oh, really. *Now?*"

"Yep, *now*. My purse only had room for two tampons. I have one left."

"Damn. Your vag has spectacular timing. Is there anything I can do?"

"I'll be sure to add 'well-timed vagina' to my résumé—right after self-starter and proficient in MS Office. There's not much we can do at this point. I can probably get through today on what I have. After that I'm gonna have to improvise."

The gas station was right across from a two-lane on-ramp that sloped upwards and then curved around to merge with a southbound highway. We crossed the street and Jeff clambered over a guardrail to scope out a patch of grass just before the on-ramp. "This works," he waved. "Come on over."

I made a move to follow him, but something caught as I slid over the galvanized steel of the guardrail. It was my dress. The embroidered hem was tangled around a bolt. By the time I realized I was caught, the damage had already been done. The air quivered with the sound of ripping fabric. My green dress was wounded. The delicately embroidered fabric had a huge, frayed gash that no amount of stitching would ever fix.

I bent over in the grass and ran the damaged cotton through my hands only to find my vision blurred with tears. The dress was impractical and it was pointless to get sentimental over an article of clothing, but I couldn't help feeling slightly bereaved. Impractical or not, the green dress encapsulated all the magic absurdity of our trip. I'd worn it every day for the last two weeks. And now I'd fucking ripped it.

Jeff missed the demise of my dress. He was a little further down the guardrail, bowed over the hitchhiking sign, thickening the ink around each letter of "Sarajevo" for better visibility. The red marker dug into the cardboard with curt, determined strokes. He was in strategy mode.

He didn't even pause to look up as I approached with torn hem in hand. "I was thinking," he said. "It might be more efficient if *you* were the one holding the sign. I'll hang back a few feet while you stand out by the road and hold out your thumb. Maybe let your hair down for a little extra sex appeal?"

It was the wrong thing to say.

"Sex appeal? *Really?*" I yelled. "You invite me on a trip with no baggage and one dress—which is now ripped, by the way—yet you also expect me to let my hair down and be *sexy* in a pair of bloody underwear with sweat running down my back. Because all women are ripe for sexual objectification, right? Maybe I should unbutton a few more buttons for maximum desirability? Or maybe I'll just strip off all my clothes and pole dance on the highway sign. Would that be efficient?"

Jeff was completely taken aback by the sheer force of my outrage. His red marker froze mid-stroke. He looked at me and then looked away, mildly abashed by his styling tips. With zero warning, I'd metamorphosed from wallflower to furious orator. It was a trick he'd never witnessed. "I'm sorry," he said after a long, simmering pause. "I didn't mean to be an asshole. Dorottya just mentioned that drivers were more likely to stop for women. I was trying to be strategic about getting us out of here . . ."

"Well, don't try," I snapped.

I glowered at him in the tall grass along the overpass. The whole world was suffocatingly still. The air, the empty road, the 2-for-1 hot dog banner hanging in the gas station window across the street. Nothing happened even when I snatched the hitchhiking sign and grudgingly held out my thumb. Sunday traffic was sparse. The few drivers who did enter the highway openly gawked at the sight of a tall cowboy in red slacks next to a sullen girl in a tailored summer dress.

We stood in the sun for an hour. No one so much as tapped the brakes. It was past noon. We hadn't made it a mile out of Budapest.

"Let's just start walking to Sarajevo," said Jeff, who had been quiet since my outburst.

"Fine," I said. It was a ridiculous idea, but I didn't have a better one.

We started up the on-ramp towards the highway with nothing except an irrational plan to head south on foot. Then, right as we reached the apex of the on-ramp, I heard a honk. A rusty Peugeot hatchback was pulling over onto the narrow on-ramp shoulder. Or rather, *mostly* onto the shoulder. The driver—a portly, fatherly-type—hopped out of the car and waved to us. He appeared to be in cheerful oblivion to the fact that the back half of his vehicle was still parked firmly in the right lane, completely exposed to oncoming traffic.

Jeff and I raced to the Peugeot. We were both giddy about our first hitch of the trip and frightened that neither of us might live long enough to enjoy it. In stumbling English, the Good Samaritan told us he was an ice cream maker on his way to gather strawberries. Ice cream explained why the Peugeot was filled with two-dozen plastic strawberry crates, which he was frantically rearranging to clear two seats. It was a high-stakes game of Tetris. My skin prickled with every *swish* of a passing car.

"Oh dear," I whispered to Jeff.

"Jesus," he said.

Jeff disappeared back down the on-ramp to flag traffic into the left lane while I stayed with Strawberry Ice Cream Man, unsure of what to do. I offered to help him pack the crates, but it was like offering a brain surgeon a hand with a lobotomy. He had a honed system. All I could do was stand on the on-ramp and pray that the emergency rescue crew wouldn't notice my bloody underwear when they peeled our crushed bodies off the highway.

. . .

It had only been a few weeks since my last car crash. When Jeff met me back in April, I owned a black 2003 Honda Civic I affectionately referred to as "Mushy." Mushy loosely resembled a functioning vehicle in the same way that grape Jolly Ranchers taste like real grapes. The front bumper was crushed. Half of the back bumper had caved in. The evil orange glow of the check engine light eternally taunted me from the dash. The air-conditioning was moody on a cool day and totally unresponsive on a hot one. Plus, the transmission was failing, which meant I reenacted the early stages of a plane crash whenever I switched from second gear to third. I was basically driving a collision with an engine. It sucked, but I was in no position to buy a new one.

Still, for all of Mushy's shortcomings, the car did manage to solve the problem of itself. It was a rainy May afternoon in Austin. The night before Jeff had driven up from Brownsville. We'd gone on our fourth date. He spent the night and made me coffee in the morning. I left him lounging in my studio and headed out to a doctor's appointment. Five minutes later, I called him, the phone shaking in my hands. *I just had an accident. Can you come get me?*

Mushy's brakes had given out on the downward slope of a steep hill. The road was slick with fresh rain and road grease. As soon as I felt the oily, gliding nothingness beneath the tires I knew I was going to hit the SUV at the stop sign in front of me. It was a calm, slow-motion moment. I'd had time to reconcile myself to the inevitable crush of impact.

No one was hurt. The SUV belonged to two Korean college students who riskily documented the fresh dent in their bumper as rush hour traffic screeched up and down the slippery hill. Mushy didn't fare so well. The front looked like a crushed candy wrapper, steam was billowing out from under the hood and the air smelled like burning rubber. There was barely enough life left for me to drive off the road and into the vacant parking lot where Jeff picked me up.

A week before our trip, the insurance company declared the car totaled and mailed me a check for $8,000—more than twice what I'd paid for it and at least four times more than what it was actually worth. Jeff and I were driving down the interstate when the insurance agent called to deliver the news. I hung up and banged my fist triumphantly on the dash. "Mushy performed a miracle! That sweet piece of shit!" After two years of either unemployment or living paycheck to paycheck on a part-time, entry-level salary, $8,000 was like winning the lottery.

"It's a sign," said Jeff with a devilish look in his eyes. "Now you can afford to go on our trip *and* quit your new job."

"You're mad," I said.

I met Jeff the same week I quit my part-time secretary job to take a full-time, work-from-home position as an iPad application reviewer for a company in Los Angeles. It was a big leap. A few months earlier I was giving myself a gold sticker every time I managed to drag my body out of bed in the morning. Now I was striking out on my own. My new boss was happy with my performance and allowed me to organize my schedule around my upcoming trip. For the first time in years I didn't have to pick up odd jobs to cover my rent. The only catch was that watching ice cubes melt was more stimulating than reviewing software apps. On paper, the job was a perfect stepping-stone back to stability. But it felt like a drab dead end. I had no reasonable explanation why—just a gut feeling.

Jeff was wholly convinced I needed to follow my gut, quit my shiny new job, and take off with him to Istanbul. Like Mushy, the rest would spontaneously figure itself out.

"It's clearly what the Mush would have wanted," he said, tapping the steering wheel.

"I would be crazy to quit," I argued. "This job is a real chance at stability. I just cleaned out my bank account for a ticket to Istanbul, which already puts me *way* over my questionable decision making quota for the year. Do you know how miserable it is to constantly be broke?"

"Well, I could help out," he offered. "It would give you some time to explore and figure things out."

I waited, expecting the punchline as we sped past mesquite-dotted cow pastures along I-10. But he was dead serious. I studied him, wonderingly, and then brushed the proposal off. "Right. So I should put my financial security in the hands of a guy who can't even commit to five minutes from now?"

"Just a thought," he said.

But even as I ran through my fears, I felt the cord of rope drawing me out towards the edge. Quitting without a plan was not advisable. The only thing I had to go on was the uncanny intuition that something was waiting for me and I had to drop everything to be ready for it.

A few days later I emailed my boss. *I've had a new opportunity come up.* I wanted to add *and I have no idea what it is*, but instead I signed off with "best wishes." There was nothing to do but watch, wait, and hope the concept of "gut intuition" was more than a spiritual conspiracy theory.

. . .

By some miracle, the Strawberry Samaritan did manage to clear two narrow canyons of space in his Peugeot before highway traffic did us in. At some point he asked where our bags were. Jeff said we didn't have any. It was good thing too—there wasn't a spare inch for anything except for our three bodies and the two-dozen empty strawberry crates.

The Strawberry Samaritan conveyed us 150 miles to the Croatian border. It was a pleasant but uneventful drive. We said our goodbyes and he headed on to his errands. At the Croatian border, an elderly language teacher picked us up and drove us to the nearest town. She said almost nothing, but the folk songs blasting out of her radio filled the silence. My legs stuck to her hot leather seats.

She dropped us in a tiny country town—more like the afterthought of a town. There was one gas station and an empty playground with faded paint. We bought a bag of exotic peanut-flavored Cheetos in the gas station and devoured them on the empty main drag, our thumbs covered in sweat and fluorescent cheese crumbs. After another round of waiting, a well-groomed Sean Connery lookalike in a sleek gray Subaru pulled up. He said he could take us to Osijek, the next major city thirty miles to the south. We hopped in.

I sat in the back. Jeff sat up front to spare me the lion's share of small talk. Sean Connery spoke a little English and all three of us were attempting to make polite conversation. We asked about his work. He informed us that he worked with wines. "Clara loves wine," said Jeff. "But I'm allergic. I get these splitting headaches after one sip. Something about the tannins."

Sean gave him an odd look, but said nothing. I tried to fill the silence by inquiring about regional grape varietals. Jeff asked about soil quality in the pastoral hills out the window. Sean seemed to know little about either topic, which was puzzling. He was also wearing military green fatigues that didn't exactly scream winemaker of the year. Finally, on the outskirts of Osijek, he jerked the car off the road and parked near a tree-lined pasture. "I show you wines," he said.

"Dorottya didn't say anything about following strangers in fields," I whispered to Jeff as Sean led us down a dirt path.

"Hold on a second . . . ," said Jeff. The path wasn't leading to rows of clipped grape vines but to a barbed wire fence with an ominous skull and bones sign. Sean Connery held his fingers to his ears and bent his shoulders, simulating a bomb blast.

Jeff and I connected the dots at exactly the same moment. "Holy shit," I said. "He works with *mines*! Not *wines*."

It was a lost in translation moment. The city of Osijek was positioned right along a strip of one of the most heavily mined areas during the 1991 Croatian War for Independence. Sean Connery was one of the contractors hired to clear mines that had been buried in the surrounding fields more than twenty years earlier.

As the three of us stood beside the field, I was overwhelmed by the utter strangeness of the scene. Everything was mixed up: the idyllic ash trees gently bending in the summer afternoon breeze, the deadly minefield just beyond the fence, Sean Connery in his military garb. It was surreal. I was on my period, standing empty-handed in a torn green dress on the side of a Croatian highway with some guy I'd met on OkCupid. What magnetic force had pulled me from Austin to here? Where would it fling me next?

CHAPTER 12 | A Problem Like Maria

I knew Maria was Jeff's type the moment I saw her waiting outside the Slavonski Brod bus terminal. She was a deer—delicate and hollow cheeked with a faraway expression and eyes that seemed unusually preoccupied with the stormy late afternoon sky above the parking lot. Her unwashed nutmeg hair hung around her face like a curtain. She flicked it out of her eyes with a wrist that was far more slender than mine—the kind you could easily encircle with thumb and forefinger. A worn knapsack leaned against her military boots. She couldn't have been much older than twenty-three.

Jeff noticed her as we walked into the terminal to buy bus tickets. It wasn't just a casual look in passing either. He stared. I could see the pistons of curiosity firing in his brain. *Which is totally fine,* I reminded myself as we stepped up to the ticket window. *Nothing wrong with being attracted to other people.* It didn't help that I wasn't feeling terribly attractive myself. My system was awash with hormones, I was sunburned, and I'd already gone through my second tampon, leaving me no choice but to fashion makeshift pads out of cheap bus station toilet paper that was so thin I could see right through it.

We'd ended up at the Slavonski Brod bus terminal after the minefield tour. Sean Connery had dropped us in the dusty city of Osijek where we put hitchhiking on hold and stopped at a café for a traditional Croatian *ćevapi* dish featuring a dozen mini-sausages doused in cream then stuffed between two round pancakes. Afterwards we drifted down an unknown boulevard in a tryptophan haze, sleepily searching for our next hitchhiking spot. It was there that Igor the tank driver picked us up.

Igor was a dark-haired, melancholy Croat stuck in a mire of circumstance. He was about my age, but the heaviness in his eyes made him look a decade older. He was eager to practice the English he'd gleaned by watching American action films: *Terminator, Top Gun, Rambo,* and James Bond. He dreamed of getting out of Osijek and going to school, but the economy was bad and the only alternative to a dead-end job was driving a tank for the army.

"I live in Osijek," he told us. "But I can take you to better place for hitchhiking." He reconsidered after checking the horizon through his windshield. "Rain is coming. Hitchhiking very bad. Better to take bus."

Igor was right. It was sunny in Osijek, but the horizon was a dark bar of clouds. The sky looked just like it had at the Hotel Gellert pools. Jeff and I didn't consult for long. Getting to Sarajevo had already been thrilling enough without the extra excitement of a summer thunderstorm. "Would you mind taking us to the bus station instead?" I said.

That's how we ended up on a rainy bus to Slavonski Brod, a small Croatian city right on the Bosnian border. That's also how we met Maria.

Jeff wasn't attracted to women with perfect Victoria's Secret figures, symmetrical faces, and teased hair. He preferred the peculiar—women who stood out in a crowd not for their raw, va-va-voom sex appeal, but for something *else*. Something alien. A naturally occurring strangeness that wasn't manufactured or painted on.

I was aware of his preferences because I possessed them myself—or at least he told me I did. My strain of beauty was strange. I had a crooked mouth and an overbite so severe that dentists swore they could only correct it by breaking my jaw open. The faraway look in Maria's eyes was often in my own, a fact that hadn't escaped Jeff. As we sat drinking beers in the waiting area, his eyes occasionally drifted from our table over to hers in a way that made my stomach tighten. It was juvenile, but I hoped she wasn't boarding our bus to Sarajevo.

"*Sada ukrcaj!*" shouted a bus driver. *Now boarding.*

"That's us," said Jeff.

I followed the brim of his sweat-stained Stetson into a crowd of passengers pooling around the entrance to a large coach. The bus to Sarajevo was like a white honeydew melon: sleek and smooth on the outside, seedy on the inside. We took our seats in a den-like interior, thick with carpet and cognac curtains. I half expected to see cigar smoke collecting in the dark baggage racks and Carlo Gambino plotting in the row across from us. Instead there was Maria. One of the last passengers to board, she floated ghostlike down the aisle, stopping only when she reached the window seat directly in front of Jeff. I sighed. *Really?* Of all the buses and all the seats, she had to choose that one.

I felt a twinge of guilt as the bus groaned away from the

station. *So what if Jeff noticed her?* He had no claim on me and I had no claim on him. Under our strict, boundary-less arrangement, both of us were technically free to pursue anyone we pleased. Jeff always gravitated towards the most intriguing people in the room, and in this case the most intriguing person just happened to be a strangely attractive woman who, through no fault of her own, had ended up in the seat in front of him. I had no legitimate reasons to dislike Maria. *Zip, zero, nada.* It wasn't like she was seducing Jeff with bedroom eyes or tattooing his name across her delicate wrists. As far as I could tell, she hadn't even registered his existence. I was being unreasonable. Paranoid, even.

My petty jealousy seemed even pettier as the bus crossed over the Sava River and into the Bosnian city of Brod. With no preface, the city's plaster façades began shifting from smooth to pockmarked. I leaned on Jeff's shoulder and stared out the window. The city was strafed during the mid-'90s Balkan War. It was a jarring scene—the juxtaposition of everyday city life beneath blatant reminders of violence.

But even Brod was nothing compared to the rainy Bosnian countryside where shelled out skeleton houses with collapsed roofs and Swiss-cheese walls dominated the rolling grassy hills for mile after mile. Jeff and I were dead silent.

I'd studied the complicated history of the Balkans in college—the death of Tito led communist Yugoslavia to violently split along ethnic fault lines—but reading about war was entirely different than witnessing the raw reality of its aftermath. Nothing in my life experience corresponded with the view out the bus window.

As a white, middle-class American woman, my exposure to violence had always been abstract and sanitized. Death was kept at a safe, orderly Fox-News distance. The only dead body I'd seen was a septuagenarian with ochre lipstick in a West Texas funeral home. I'd been to historic battle sites— the Alamo and Gettysburg—but those have long since been cleaned up and memorialized with paintings, brass plaques, and guided audio tours. Here in Bosnia and other Balkan countries, the memory of war was still visceral and fresh, the soil was still being combed for land mines, and a certain pathos was visible in the eyes of everyone over thirty.

The long parade of skeleton homes ended only after the sun set and it was too dark to see. I was in no mood to chat. I needed quiet to process the bleak scenes that had seeped out of the landscape and under my skin. Jeff was affected by the view too, but he cycled through emotions faster and tended to focus on whatever was directly in front of him, which, in this case, was Maria. I could tell he was waiting for the chance to strike up a conversation. His window of opportunity opened when the bus shuddered to a halt in the middle of the road. A wave of nervous whispers rippled through the seats as the lights flickered then died, plunging the bus into rainy darkness.

Jeff made his move. "Guess we're going to have to push this bus to Sarajevo," he said to no one in particular. Maria giggled and turned around in her seat. And that was that. Her name was Maria, she told him over the headrest. She was fascinating, of course—a painter from a bohemian French family on her way to take the entrance exams at the art school in Sarajevo. I closed my eyes and folded my hands, a silent protest against their flirty banter. When Maria dug in her bag and offered us chocolates, I said I wasn't hungry— a blatant lie.

. . .

I was on intimate terms with anxiety and panic, but jealousy was a fresh addition to my emotional repertoire. In past relationships I'd indulged in the occasional petty eye roll over mentions of the ex, but, for some reason, that was the extent of it. I'd never experienced the hard lump welling up in my throat, or the overpowering desire to slam doors until the handles shuddered, or the hot rush of insecurity.

And then I met Jeff.

The first sparks of jealousy caught me completely off guard. It was like a dragon had been sleeping in my chest for the last twenty-five years and was just now waking up. I'd always assumed I was above "that sort of thing." I took my relationship aspirations from the bohemians: Georgia O'Keeffe's marriage to Alfred Stieglitz and Simone de Beauvoir's lifelong connection to Jean-Paul Sartre (though neither of those arrangements was particularly blissful). I was the one who'd tried to coax ex-boyfriends into avant-garde open relationships, the one who clung to my page-worn copy of *Sex at Dawn,* and the one who could always be counted on to lift a suspicious eyebrow at the institution of monogamy. I'd memorized a list of saccharine platitudes about the limitless nature of human love and desire. (*Just because you fall in love with one person doesn't mean your supply of love suddenly dries up! There are as many permutations of love as there are people on the planet!*)

Even worse was the unavoidable truth that, out of the two of us, Jeff had far more legitimate reasons to be jealous than I did. I was the only one who'd taken advantage of our agreement to pursue whatever (or whomever) we desired. I was the only one who'd slept with someone else.

The deed took place two weeks after I met Jeff. I was heady over our glorious new openness, and when a tall, dark admirer asked me out on a date, I jumped at the chance to take my freedom out for a test spin. Jeff was back in Brownsville, but he was on board. He told me to go out and do what I wanted to do. So I did. The tall, dark guy took me to a concert, we flirted over beers, and then I invited him back to my place for the proverbial "nightcap."

Sadly, my intellectual view of sexual liberty failed to live up to the sweaty reality. The sex wasn't great. I wasn't at all sure that slipping off my underwear was what I truly wanted to do—it felt more like what I *should* want to do given the circumstances. During the act, I stared at the paint constellations in my popcorn ceiling, waiting for it to be over. When he asked if he could stay the night, I shook my head, *no*. I asked him to leave. With the door bolted shut, I sat naked on the edge of the bed, wishing it had been Jeff instead. Then I got in the shower and scrubbed my skin a ragged, blistery red, as if enough soap could wash the last hour away.

Jeff was composed when I shyly broke the news a few

mornings later. A flash of surprise briefly flickered across his face and then he just took another sip of coffee and smiled. He said he guessed as much.

"I was walking across a parking lot when you were with him. It was right at 11 p.m. The weather was totally calm. Then, out of nowhere, this crazy wind picked up and hurled three orange and white traffic barriers *right* at me. They must have weighed 100 pounds each. I knew something was up."

The fact that he had so calmly processed the thought of me being naked with someone else made me feel even worse about my own rising sense of vulnerability. Maybe love was a boundless well, but it was also a complex, emotional labyrinth unless everyone involved was an ego-less bodhisattva soaring lotus position through the stratosphere—which I clearly wasn't.

The more I thought about it, the more I realized I'd laughably oversimplified the realities of an "undefined relationship." Jeff seemed to be open to any sort of tangling in the sheets, but I was considerably less bohemian than I'd first assumed. Unless we were going for a bacchanalian free-for-all, it seemed prudent to get some advice on the practical mechanics of our arrangement.

When Jeff wasn't around, I reverted back to my old habit of obsessive Googling. Only this time instead of obsessing over the meaning of life, I was obsessing over which flavor of ambiguous modern relationship I'd unwittingly signed myself up for.

The results were surprising. I'd long since abandoned the Christian assumption that a proper relationship could only happen between one woman and one man joined in holy matrimony forever, but I hadn't realized just how many options for configuring a relationship exist or how structured some of the more avant-garde arrangements tend to be. There are some couples who agree to strict "don't ask, don't tell" sexual policies, but even those often have caveats (always use protection, no falling in love, no sex with mutual friends, not in our bed).

While the mention of "non-monogamy" or "open relationships" might conjure up scenes of unbridled debauchery, the reality is far more likely to involve extensive communication and clearly established boundaries. In the polyamorous community, "love between many" can take an endless number of forms. It is so multifaceted that it has its own glossary of terms, definitions, and colloquialisms; words that bring to mind complex carpentry, like closed triad, polyfidelity, and hinge. Far from being ambiguous free-for-alls, nontraditional relationships are often highly structured by necessity. Two people is hard enough—successfully adding more pieces to the puzzle requires care and planning.

During one of my research sprees, I stumbled across a particularly astounding feat of romance—a San Francisco tech manager who maintained a fiancé, a girlfriend, and two boyfriends and used Google calendar to keep her dating schedule on point. I was awed by the sheer logistics. Did she spend the night at her partners' houses? If so, how many times a week? How many of the gritty details did she share with her fiancé? What did she do when someone felt uncomfortable? How often did she communicate with everyone involved? How the hell did she manage all these emotional entanglements on top of a full-time career?

By the end of my research spree, I was more bewildered than when I'd started. There was no official consensus on the optimal relationship arrangement. Every configuration is susceptible to jealousy. Sexuality is a complex spectrum where some people appear to be better suited for monogamy than others, and statistics show that open relationships fail just as often as strictly monogamous ones. After hours of feverish research, the only conclusion I could reasonably assert was that all romantic relationships require a brave plunge into vulnerability—no matter what particular arrangement suits your fancy.

. . .

I was spearing edamame with my fork when Jeff casually mentioned another woman from OkCupid. We were sitting at a cheap downtown Austin café. I froze, unable to look up from my lunch salad. As he started in with the details I became newly fascinated by the perfect green roundness of each edamame pod in my bowl. *Edamame in a feta avalanche.* Single mom who worked at a local marketing firm. *Two edamame in a spinach cavern.* She'd contacted him, not the other way around. *Edamame speckled with pepper.* Might be a good connection for the Dumpster Project. *Half an edamame drowning in vinaigrette.* Lunch tomorrow. Nothing would happen—probably. *Probably?*

"OkCupid? That's . . . really great." I managed to choke out the words as I set my fork down, appetite erased.

I'd deleted my OkCupid account exactly seven days after I opened it. Managing the tidal wave of propositions that opened with "hey baby, how u doing?" had quickly escalated into a shitty part-time job filled with sex fiends and overly earnest graduate students. (I pulled the cord after receiving an ardent poem that read, *"Your profile was like breaking through to a clearing in a dense wood, sunlit and sunbathed, quietly going about the business of replenishment that's characteristic of a mid-May spring day."*)

Unlike me, Jeff had left his OkCupid account active. I knew that. He hadn't hid it from me. Leaving the account open was aligned with the "Keeping It Simple" speech he gave to every woman in his post-divorce phase. *Just so you know, I'm seeing other people and you should feel free to do the same.* He'd never officially given me the speech, but it was waiting in the wings, always hovering. And hell, I'd practically given him the same spiel. My racing pulse and newfound edamame fascination was completely unwarranted. He was trying to do me a favor by being transparent. Neither of us knew what we were doing.

"Are you okay?" he said, running his finger around the edge of his salad bowl, then licking it. "Your face looks kinda . . . gray."

"I'm fine," I lied. "It's just . . . a little hard."

"I get that," he said slowly. "But I still want to meet her. This might be a connection worth investigating and I'm not going to turn it down out of fear. Plus, you went out with . . ."

"I know, *I know*," I said, waving my hand to cut him off. "I fucked him. And I wish I hadn't because this open-ended *whatever* is so much harder than I expected. I mean, I know how to handle intellectual unknowns, but this is different. This is physical. It's flesh and blood and lust. I'm scared you're going to ride off as soon as a smarter, sexier, more-accomplished woman messages you on OkCupid. And I feel guilty for being scared. I really hate that my ideals aren't matching up with my emotions."

He began pensively arranging a crumpled napkin, used salt packet, and plastic fork inside his empty salad bowl. "I thought this is what *you* wanted to try," he said.

"It is," I said softly. "Be careful what you ask for, I guess."

We split up after lunch. Jeff disappeared. His guard was up. He was a wild dog backing away, afraid of being caged. I paced under the skyscraper shadows of downtown Austin, fueled by hot jealousy. An irrational tape straight out of a trashy romance novel looped over and over in my brain.

I imagined Jeff and the sexy marketing exec sharing the pad Thai lunch special. They'd start off discussing the subtleties of social media campaigns. Then she'd confide that she'd been feeling a little lonely. Her pressed silk blouse would be unbuttoned just enough to be unprofessional. Her fire engine red lipstick would leave a seductive mark on her napkin. They'd finish off the spring rolls. She'd purse her lips and say, "Oh! What a coincidence. My 2 o'clock just cancelled." Then he'd whisk her off to a cheap hotel. He'd rip the silk blouse open. The buttons would spill across the bed. I'd be the furthest thing from his mind.

The bodice-ripping fantasy clenched my stomach, but—then again—so did the thought of pulling back on our relationship. I wasn't ready to do that. Not yet, at least. My fear was strong, but the desire to see where things went with Jeff was even stronger. By the time the sky deepened into a dark violet I was standing in front of the Texas State Capitol, attempting to steady my nerves on the same tiled star where we'd met a few weeks earlier. Around me, tourists posed in front of ornamental cannons. The floodlights beneath the flagpoles switched on. The crickets began to sing. My phone buzzed. It was Jeff. *Where are you?* I waited ten minutes to give him the impression that I was *busy doing other things.* Then I hesitantly texted him a picture of the star. *On my way,* he wrote.

My eyes began to well the moment I saw him coming towards me under the streetlamps, smiling his coyote smile.

Without saying a word, he grabbed my hand and led me down to the dark Capitol lawn where he pulled me down on top of him into the musky grass. I started to bawl. He wrapped my heaving shoulders tightly into his arms, and laughed, laughed, laughed. A wild dog howling at the moon. He was howling at the universe, still daring it to try something he hadn't seen, something that would scare him off. We were a grassy tangle of limbs, tears, and glee.

"Everything is going to be okay," he whispered. "No matter what."

"I know," I said. "I'm just afraid it's going to hurt."

. . .

Of course we didn't come to any decisive conclusions that night. Jeff went on the lunch date. Nothing happened other than lunch. My jealousy gradually diminished. There weren't any more blood-rushing crescendos until I spotted Maria on the bus to Sarajevo—or rather, on the bus *trying* to make it to Sarajevo.

After the first engine failure, the bus continued to flatline in the road every ten miles. With each shuddering halt we collectively held our breath, wondering if *this* might be the time the engine refused to resuscitate, stranding us in the middle of a Bosnian highway without any taillights. Somehow, the driver always managed to coax it back to life. A communal cheer traveled down the thick-curtained aisles each time the cab lights flickered back on and the bus hobbled a little further down the road. It was nice, actually, to observe the camaraderie of strangers (minus Jeff and Maria).

"Would you like to see some of my work?" she asked him.

He nodded eagerly. "Hell yeah!"

I stared at him pointedly as she pulled out an art portfolio and handed it over the seat back with her porcelain wrists. "I'm so nervous about my exam tomorrow," she confessed. "I haven't slept in two days. I took some ecstasy before the bus."

Ecstasy. That's why she was so entranced by the sky over the bus station. Drugs also explained why the two greasy-haired Euro-frat types sitting across the aisle had covertly slipped her a bottle of glue a few minutes earlier. I felt a wicked flush of satisfaction as Jeff flipped through her portfolio, cringing. Maria was no Caravaggio. There were stained-glass flowers shaded with what looked like crayons, a homework doodle, and a "portrait" featuring a morass of pencil strokes that loosely suggested a man on a couch holding a lonely, shriveled carrot on a dinner platter. *Or was that his penis?*

"That's my boyfriend," she said shyly. "He's on the couch holding a plate with the joint he just rolled."

"Wow. It really captures his . . . *platter,*" said Jeff, struggling to keep a straight face.

I hoped the weed-carrot signaled a swift end to his infatuation with Maria the Painter. But he surprised me. "Hey, so you should stay with us," he told her. "I mean, if your host doesn't show. It's past midnight so we're probably going to have to crash in a hostel. You can just stay in our room." He turned to me. "Is that cool?"

"Umm . . . *sure,*" I said, feeling my pulse begin to rocket. *You will play this cool. You will play this cool.* But I wasn't cool. Hot rage was flooding my system. How *dare* he do this right in front of me?

I imagined Jeff waiting until I was asleep to sneak away to Maria's bunk bed and quietly ravish her into the wee hours of the morning with cheap paintbrushes strewn around their sweaty, naked limbs. I imagined her pale wrists entwined around his neck and the exotic French words she'd whisper into his ear. The irrational tape was back, looping through my head at a deafening volume. *I look disgusting. Of course he wants to be with her. He knows I'm uncomfortable, but he doesn't care because he's only interested in himself. She probably knows sex positions I could only dream of.*

As far as I was concerned, the experiment was over. I wanted to slip off the dying bus and disappear into the night, away from the bombed out Bosnian countryside and back to Austin, back to my houseplants and the safe, solid boundaries of my 385-square-foot studio. I would put my heart back in its box and swear off experimental soul mates. I was ready. It was time to run.

CHAPTER 13 | Yin Yang

I woke up alone in the top bunk of an empty hostel room lined with three bunks. Jeff had slept in the bunk beneath me, but at some point he'd disappeared. The only record of his presence was a pile of rumpled sheets. No note. No stuff. He was just gone.

I half wondered if the hostel bunk bed marked the final resting place of our grand affair with the unknown. Maybe Jeff had finally reached the limit of his short-lived attention span and was in search of a sparkly new toy. Maybe he was down at the university, waiting for Maria to emerge from her art exam in a post-ecstasy haze. It was possible. She'd scrawled her contact info down in his notebook as our dying bus lurched into Sarajevo an hour after midnight. At least she didn't end up in our hostel room. Her host, a dark-haired college girl, was waiting in the foggy parking lot despite the three-hour delay.

"Pardon me, are you Maria?" she asked as I stepped off the bus.

"Oh, no," I said. "But she's coming." *Please take her to a galaxy far, far away.*

Jeff hugged Maria goodbye. I wished her "good luck" with a tone that was a lot closer to "peace out, *bitch*." Then Jeff and I turned to each other. "Guess we should head to the hostel," he said between yawns.

I couldn't believe he was yawning. His mouth was a gaping chasm filled with careless, oblivious "Os". He was oblivious to my panic, oblivious to the poison darts shooting out of my retinas, oblivious to the fact that he'd just spent an entire bus ride casually flirting with a beautiful French woman two feet from my nose. He simply didn't care.

"Yeah, whatever," I said, mentally capping the sentence with "asshole."

A taxi driver with a damp cigarette dangling out of the side of his mouth conveyed us through the misty cobblestone streets of Sarajevo. At the hostel, I crawled into the top bunk without speaking. A tiny part of me hoped Jeff might break the stony silence, but there was nothing. He made no move to join me and I certainly wasn't about to wave the olive branch.

It was the first night we slept apart.

The next morning I woke up feeling like a pulverized cricket on a windshield—especially after I realized Jeff was gone. There was nothing to do but crawl into the shower and sit under the hot stream, scrubbing my blood-stained underwear with the little ivory round of hostel soap. I inhaled the detergent steam as if it could help me catch my bearings. *Is he coming back? Do I even care?*

I would leave, I decided. I would wander through the city instead of sitting around waiting around for him. Leaving is what any self-respecting woman would do. After the shower, I combed my wet hair, stocked up on toilet paper for makeshift tampons, and packed my handful of possessions back into my purse. *Wallet. Toothbrush. Deodorant.* I'd developed a tight system by that point. Every object had a place.

The doorknob turned right as I clipped my purse shut and swung it over my shoulder. Jeff marched into the room. He was holding a plastic bag and beaming like a sunflower.

"You're here . . . ," I said, confused.

He gave me an odd look. "Yeah, why wouldn't I be? I brought you a present! Hope you like it, because it took me all morning to track down." He drew a box of fifty sanitary pads out of the bag and presented it to me proudly, like it was a bouquet of roses. "I tried to get tampons, but they don't have any here. You know how I found that out?"

"Umm, how?" I whispered.

He made an obscene hole-poking motion with his finger. "I went from shop to shop making hand motions for 'tampon.' No one had any. Finally, this one shop owner was like, 'Hey man, it's called a tampon and you won't find any here.' So, I got you pads instead."

"Thanks. That was really thoughtful." I said the words in slow-motion.

"It's a testament of my affection. How many guys would wander through Sarajevo on a tampon hunt?"

"Not many, I guess."

I was confused by his attentiveness. Jeff hadn't taken off at all. He wasn't doggedly pursuing Maria. He'd spent the morning earnestly wandering the streets for feminine products. Why would he go to that length if he didn't care about anyone except himself?

"I can't wait for you to see Sarajevo," he said, still beaming, as if last night had never happened. "You're going to fall in love."

. . .

My mood was slightly softened by the feminine product peace offering. I stuffed as many pads as I could fit into my dress pockets and then summoned a weak smile as we walked out into the cloudy morning light. Jeff was right about one thing at least—Sarajevo was about to steal my heart. The city was a foggy jewel ensconced on all sides by sharp, forested hills and the peaks of the Dinaric Alps just beyond. It was chilly and crisp. I wrapped my scarf tightly around my arms as we headed down the hilly, cobblestone streets towards Baščaršija, the Sarajevo old town.

Before the 1990s Bosnian War and its bloody ethnic power struggles, Sarajevo had once been called the Jerusalem of Europe, a testament to a city where you could walk to an orthodox church, a mosque, a synagogue, and a cathedral, all within a few blocks' radius. And despite the propaganda wars and the massacres and the deep rents between Orthodox Serbs, Muslim Bosniaks, and Roman Catholic Croats, Sarajevo's resiliency hearkens back to a much older tradition of tolerance and laid-back camaraderie.

The city was once an important trade stop for merchants along the Silk Road. That meeting point is still visible in the Ottoman domes that hover over posh Italian restaurants; the terra-cotta-tiled cafés where Muslim men bow their heads over morning cups of coffee; and the nearby corner where Franz Ferdinand, the Austro-Hungarian archduke, fell to the floor of his car, gasping, "It is nothing," after being shot in the neck with the bullet that cascaded Europe into the First World War.

Before breakfast, Jeff and I stopped in a square where hundreds of pigeons flocked around one of the most iconic symbols of Sarajevo—the Sebilj, a geometric Ottoman fountain constructed out of carved wood and topped with a pigeon-perch, copper dome that had weathered turquoise with age. According to local legend, anyone who drank from the waters of the public fountain was destined to return to Sarajevo once again. "We should take our side-by-side picture here," Jeff said. He flew over to recruit a passerby without waiting to hear my usual protest about the dozens of photo ops he'd already subjected me to.

At least the snap was fast. We reviewed the picture afterwards. There were the foggy, forested hills, the turquoise dome of the Sebilj, Jeff squinting on the left, and me on the right, clutching my floral scarf with a grim smile. If we'd studied the picture a little closer, we would have also noticed the half-dozen white pads preparing to stage an escape from my dress pocket. But we didn't notice.

However, someone else did. I felt a poking tap on my shoulder. It was a hunched elderly man in a cap pointing a wrinkled finger to the cobblestones in front of the Sebilj, which were littered with a Hansel-and-Gretel trail of snowy cotton pads. My hand flew to my mouth. *This was the price of taking no bags.* I was adorning the revered symbol of Sarajevo with feminine products intended to absorb menstrual blood. Mortified, I hopped around, sending flocks of pigeons into the air as I scooped up the pads and stuffed them back into my pockets. Jeff giggled as he helped retrieve the wayward pads.

It was hard to be so angry after that, though I did try to maintain a bit of residual angst. Jeff made it even harder when he bought a bag of birdseed from a gypsy-looking woman in a long navy skirt and a bandana covered in roses. He skipped around the Sebilj Square tossing showers of yellow corn above the crowd of greedy, cooing pigeons waddling at his feet.

(It's actually quite difficult to be outraged while observing a fat, bobbing pigeon as it blithely lumbers across the sidewalk. Pigeons, while not exactly the Einsteins of the winged phylum, are affable, simple-minded birds totally content with waddling around in funny, pecking circles.

Wallowing in anger in front of one is like trying to rub your stomach while patting your head and hopping on one foot—inevitably, you just give up and laugh.)

Still, while my mood had lifted enough to enjoy Sarajevo, I wasn't any less preoccupied with the Maria debacle (and the increasingly apparent pitfalls of our "anything goes" philosophy.) We needed to talk. But we also needed to turn right around and get on another bus headed south to Dubrovnik, Croatia, where our flight to Scotland was scheduled to leave the next morning. For the first time on the trip, Jeff was reluctant to leave a city. I was too—we were moving so fast I could hardly enjoy the destinations—but after a breakfast and a stroll through the old alleys of Baščaršija, we had no choice but to leave. We were on a bus out of Sarajevo before the morning fog had even begun to burn off.

. . .

I didn't bring Maria up right away. Jeff put his earbuds in and closed his eyes, giving me a chance to gather my thoughts as the bus wound south through Herzegovina. Out the window the mountains of Sarajevo shifted into high ravines. The pale jade Neretva River snaked through the valley, far below the cliff-hugging road. I half wished I could dive under the surface and avoid the impending confrontation, but there was no way I could hide from this one. I took a deep breath and tapped on Jeff's knee.

He pulled out his earbuds. I could faintly hear the lilting chorus of "Back on the Chain Gang" by The Pretenders. "What's up?"

"I need to ask you something," I said.

"Okay . . . ," he said, sitting up a little straighter in his chair.

"I need to know what happened last night."

He stared at me, filing through his memory and coming up blank. "Last night?"

"Yeah, last night on the bus?" I spat out the word bus like an accusation.

"What about it?"

"You were tripping all over yourself to talk to Maria, the marginally skilled painter."

"Wait. What?" he said, surprised. "*That's* what you're upset about?"

"Yeah. Of course that's what I'm upset about," I said, trying to keep my volume low. "You flirted with her the *entire* trip while I melted into a bloody, hormonal mess. Then you invited her back to our room."

To my great annoyance, Jeff had a smile playing around the corners of his mouth. "So, let me get this straight. You thought I fell in love with Maria and was plotting to get her back to the hostel so we could—what—have a filthy, drug-fueled threesome?"

"Well . . . something like that. It was obvious that you were attracted to her. Don't you dare deny it."

"Okay," he confessed. "I noticed her when we walked into the bus station and I thought she looked intriguing. Then when she sat right in front of me, I was like, 'hmmm, interesting.' But after we exchanged a few sentences the mystery was gone. She was just another aristocratic hipster trying to work out her trust fund baggage."

"So you weren't planning something kinky at the hostel?"

"God! No!" he groaned. "I honestly felt bad that she had no place to stay. She kept mentioning she was worried, so I just offered to let her crash with us. Why would you think I was trying to bang some girl from the bus?"

A wave of righteous indignation burst out of my chest. "Well, I dunno. Why on earth *would* I think that? Maybe it's because everything between us is so goddamn undefined! One second you're proposing to me on the beach and the next you're warning me that anything can happen at any time. I'm constantly bracing myself for whatever that 'anything' is. And I have no idea. We just met! I have no idea if you're capable of running off with a mediocre French painter. I mean, you ran off with me, the former mental case."

Jeff's smile hardened. "Oh."

"Look, this whole undefined experiment is great in theory—especially if you're single with zero attachments—but in practice it makes me feel vulnerable, like I'm constantly on the edge of a cliff. How do I know that you doing what you truly want to do isn't going to feel like shit?"

He frowned. "We *don't* know, but I thought that uncertainty is what we set out to test."

"It is! And at first I was totally down, but—the thing is—I didn't expect to feel this connection with you. Joining OkCupid was just a lark, you know? I wasn't looking for anything serious. And now there's this weird, magical thing between us."

"Okay . . ." he said slowly. "So what are you suggesting?"

"I don't know what I'm suggesting," I said, feeling a surge of words building on my tongue. "I'm just throwing stuff out. Like, I don't think I'm entirely on board with the 'do what you truly want to do' school of thought. Not without a little more nuance. There has to be an anchor in the wide-open space.

Otherwise, 'doing what you truly want' isn't an authentic attempt at exploration—it's just another hyper-individualistic credo masquerading as something grand. I mean we're all gung ho about pursuing personal freedom, but why do we want it? If we never constructively apply it to something beyond ourselves, and if it doesn't deepen our sense of connection and humanity, then what's the point?"

"Okay. And what do you think the anchor is?" he asked, pensively.

"Well, I'm sitting next to you on a Bosnian bus, so clearly I believe in following my inner gravitational pull, but I think the pull also has to be informed by a thoughtful consideration of how my choices affect the well-being of others."

"So, like awareness, basically?" he said, trying to follow my rambling train of thought.

"Well, yeah," I said. "I mean, think about it. It's a radical act for me to pour my heart out to you. It's risky for me to make myself emotionally vulnerable without any expectations of the same in return. If you don't treat it like the radical gift that it is, then why should I wrestle with the anxiety, the jealousy, and the vulnerability? Why should I open myself up if you forget my face as soon as I leave the room? It's a fucking Caesar's Palace Buffet out there."

"Hmmm," he said thoughtfully.

"And look, I get it. You've made it clear from the start that you need a lot of freedom to feel like you're operating at your optimum potential. I respect that. But I have needs too and they are different, but just as valid. It might not be hard for you to let go of definition in a relationship, but it's pretty damn hard for me. I need you to know that I'm really putting myself out there. I need you to respect that vulnerability. If you can't, then it's been fun, but I think I'm out."

My monologue ended right as the bus to Dubrovnik popped out along the blue sweep of the Croatian coast. I was surprised by the force of my own words. It was the first time I'd expressed a new, post-recovery realization: *I am brave, but not boundary-less.* After coming back to life, I'd emerged hungry for life. I shot out the front door running. Crashed my car. Quit my job. Jumped on a plane with Jeff. All under the vague assumption that this wild, new lightness would somehow suspend me above the trials of ordinary life like a plane gliding above the choppy cumulus. Who needed boundaries in a world where each moment flowed seamlessly into the next?

It was a rude surprise, then, to find myself boundless in one moment and burning with jealousy the next. What was this weakness, this newly burgeoning desire for boundaries? Enlightenment download error!

I had no guidebook, no wise sage pointing the way. I wasn't aware that no deeply transformative process is complete without a gradual returning to the ordinary world. After two years of traversing the abyss, I'd emerged with hard-won revelation. Epiphany! Rebirth! It was exhilarating, but it still wasn't curtain call. After exiting the underworld I still had to return to earth.

The intensity of an inner awakening can't be sustained indefinitely. It's too bright. It's too raw and overpowering for a world where you live in a body and have to pull out the garbage cans on trash day, and communicate in complete sentences, and maintain functioning relationships with the multitude of humans around you. Slowly, gradually, you return to earth with your revelation bottled, a potent elixir that you carry home with you to laundromats, airport security lines, corner stores, and cubicles.

Coming back to life didn't mean my old self had been annihilated in the aftershock of a mystical atom bomb. It didn't mean I had shucked off my need for protective boundaries like a dry snakeskin. I was still my same sensitive self, struggling to figure things out; struggling to strike the right balance between cliff jumps and spaces of refuge; struggling to bottle my elixir and bring it home. No one tells you that returning to earth can be such a bumpy ride.

. . .

"How long have you had all that marinating up there?" asked Jeff. He had listened patiently throughout. I was suddenly shy now that it was his turn to speak.

"A while," I said sheepishly. "Okay, weeks."

"Jesus, I'm glad you finally broke and said something. You're not exactly the first woman to inform me that I'm difficult."

"There's a shock."

"Look, dating me is probably always going to be synonymous with a certain degree of unpredictability, but I want you to know that I respect you and I respect the gravity of what we're trying to do. And you also need to know that even though I project this wild-card swagger, I'm nowhere near as risky and unpredictable as you seem to think."

"Oh, is that right?" I said skeptically.

"Yeah, it is." He stared out the bus window towards the blue coast, hesitantly fiddling with the band around his notebook. "I haven't told you this, but when we met I ended contact with the other women I was seeing before. There's something special between us, and I really want to see where it leads. Even when it's hard, and confusing, and you think I'm trying to plot a threesome with a girl who's high on glue fumes."

The disclosure hung in the air for a few seconds as I processed my shock. In Jeff's current Kerouacian phase, admitting that he wasn't looking to "hang out" with anyone else was the equivalent of swearing off the drink. It was a significant gesture. Without my knowledge he'd been secretly entertaining the slim possibility that a partnership could enhance freedom instead of weighing it down. He wasn't totally sold or anything. But he was open.

The show of vulnerability immediately lifted my rage over Maria's tiny wrists. I took a breath and looked him in the eyes. "I'd be lying if I said I didn't want to see where this leads, too. But dammit sometimes you make me want to run."

"You can run," said Jeff, sliding his arm around me as the bus took another sharp curve along the coast. "But you're not getting off that easy. We're mixed up in something now. Even if you take off, we'll just end up bumping right back into each other at some random oak."

CHAPTER 14 | Ethereal Gain

Dubrovnik, Croatia, was the calm after the emotional storm—albeit a peculiar calm. The maritime city's romantic reputation as the Pearl of the Adriatic hadn't gone unnoticed by the behemoth cruise ships docked on the outskirts of town or Easy Jet, which shuttled in melatonin-deprived Brits and Scandinavians desperate for palm trees, mitten-free Mediterranean climes, and as many flavors of gelato as there were pastel Ralph Lauren polos.

It was easy to see the appeal. Dubrovnik's Old Town was a fairytale walled medieval fortress perched right on the clear, aquamarine waters of the Dalmatian Coast. From the surrounding hills, the Old Town looked like a terra-cotta nest looped by a ribbon of turrets and stonewalls. Like Sarajevo, Dubrovnik had also been wounded during the Balkan War, but the only remaining signs of the eight-month Yugoslav

National Army siege were the bright orange patches where new terra-cotta tiles patched shell-damaged roofs.

To zoom in, however, was a different experience altogether. "What a trip," said Jeff as we strolled into the Old Town over a moat-like castle bridge and through the imposing stone mouth of Pile Gate.

"It's like a medieval Disneyland," I said. And it was. The Stradun, the main avenue, was choked with tourists snapping selfies, gelato cones in hand. They were posing not with Mickey Mouse, but with historical performers promenading through the crowds in elaborate Renaissance costumes. Unlike Disneyland, Dubrovnik stopped short of fake building façades and plastic boulders embedded with audio speakers announcing a sale in the gift shop. The polished plazas; the stone fountains where spring water splashed out of carved gargoyle mouths; the cool, Gothic halls of the Dominican friary; and the opulent, baroque flourishes of Saint Blaise Church were all part of a proud history dating back to the Medieval Era when Dubrovnik was a progressive maritime port among the likes of Venice and Ancona.

Both Jeff and I instinctively turned away from the crowded Luža Square, where a full orchestra was assembling for the opening ceremony of the annual Dubrovnik

Summer Festival. Instead, we fled up one of the many narrow staircases that threaded like paved veins up, up, up through terrace after terrace of cobblestone villas and leafy, shaded alleys. All the staircases eventually dead-ended into the thick fortress bulwarks, and that's where we settled: at the base of a turret, far above the distant melee of plaza, looking over a sweep of terra-cotta roofs and, beyond that, a blue stripe of sea. It was quiet. Cigarette butts and empty bottles were scattered across the ground, speaking to nights of intoxicated abandon above the cityscape. It was less of a tourist destination and more of a secret make-out spot.

Jeff set his Stetson on the steps and we climbed into each other's arms at the foot of the turret. Neither one of us spoke. We didn't need to. By some broken bus miracle the bond between us had strengthened over the last twenty-four hours instead of collapsing. When all the layers of uncertainty and risk were peeled away, we still had a solid kernel seed that was ripe with possibility. I had no idea what—if anything—would grow, but in that moment it was good. I was safe and warm. The storm was over. . . .

In Texas, there's an unearthly calm that always follows the black rage of a summer thunderstorm. The landscape is utterly subdued. The grass glitters and sweats. The air is muggy with the iron scent of damp soil. Unlucky tree branches lie in the street next to pools of rain and stringy, drowned earthworms. In the creeks, the wild cane is bowed all the way over after flash floods sweep through the ditches, leaving muddy Gatorade bottles and Hershey's wrappers in their wake. Most surprising though, is the clear blue sky draped above the soaking world—a sky so calm you could be forgiven for doubting the storm had ever struck at all.

After nearly two years of mental storms, I too had gradually come to know that calm. All it took was hitting the bottom end of despair. Total despair is a funny thing: it's easy to get lost in, but its finality can also set you free. In the novel *Life of Pi*, the main character is a boy lost at sea on a lifeboat with a 450-pound Bengal tiger, his only companion. He calculates his odds of survival (they aren't promising) and then declares: "You might think I lost all hope at that point. I did. And as a result I perked up and felt much better."

My Bengal tiger moment was a hot August afternoon when I collapsed on my bedroom rug and decided that, after so many months of desperate flailing, I had reached the end of my rope. I was done. I didn't care if I was "normal" or not. If I was truly mad—fine. I would be the best madwoman I could possibly be. If I was anxious every moment until I died—fine. I could function in spite of fear. If I consumed nothing but peanut-butter-jelly sandwiches for every meal of my life—fine. I would stock up on jars of extra-crunchy Jif. If I was never certain of one goddamn thing in the entire universe—fine. I would simply be unenlightened. The point was: whatever this relentless fear was, I was done fighting it. I was hoisting the white flag of surrender and letting go.

Letting go meant calling off my quest for the Holy Grail of Meaning. I still had no idea what the point of existence was. For all my searching, I'd accumulated zero truly concrete reasons as to why I should get out of bed in the morning. I was simply going to proceed without knowing. And if there was some great Oz in the sky sternly waiting for me to accomplish big meaningful things that would justify my use of oxygen and confirm my inherent value as a human being— well, then, he was just going to have to make do with me, a madwoman with peanut butter breath.

If the only thing I did for the rest of my life was treat others kindly, file manila folders, and sit on the porch watching the grass grow it would be enough. It had to be. I did the math. The number of people who actually achieve a significant legacy is trifling compared to the vast number who go from birth to death living relatively unremarkable lives (at least on the surface). And maybe that wasn't the failure I'd been conditioned to believe. Maybe there was something to be said in praise of an outwardly unremarkable life. Maybe there were deep, everyday forms of magic that had nothing to do with profound accomplishments or a Twitter feed that resonated down through the ages.

Nothing changed at first. I continued drifting through the void, as bewildered as ever. During the day I anxiously filed paperwork. At night I scrawled aimless bits of poetry at my kitchen table. I went through stacks of peanut-butter-jelly sandwiches on paper towel rectangles. I assumed this was it.

But as I fully gave myself to the anxiety, and the plainness of paperwork and plum Smucker's jelly, something began to quicken. I was like the prickly pear blossoms in my grandmother's Arizona backyard. Spiky green buds, big as your thumb, that slowly press open with the morning sun, revealing a hint of the lush, riot yellow bloom inside. The unfurling never happens all at once, but slowly, quietly, over the course of days. The hard casing of the prickly pear bud softens into a pale swirled floret, which in turn splits into a cascade of petals hungry for the sun.

My unfurling began with stillness. Instead of sprinting from terror or trying to karate chop the emptiness away, I set out a welcome mat. If I was going to be mad, I might as well acquaint myself with madness. It was an open house for monsters and I turned none away. I sat breathing in and out, sometimes for hours, as a parade of pronged horns, sharp claws, and hungry jaws moved past, invisible bodies breathing hot against my neck.

In the beginning, I often felt as if I were seconds away from being totally consumed. But over time it became clear that while the physical sensations of terror, rage, and loneliness felt deadly, they weren't actually capable of eating me alive. If I breathed long enough, every sensation eventually ran its course and passed, shifting into something different. There were days when waves of emptiness forced me to run to the bathroom, kneel at the toilet, and gag. But even then, I wiped my mouth and returned to my seat. Back to my breath. *Turn nothing away*, I reminded myself.

After a few months, my attitude towards the shadows began to soften. They weren't hideous beasts so much as painful energies trapped in my body. Anxiety was curled in my gut. Emptiness lived along the exposure of my spine. Anger had settled in the tightness of my shoulder and the clench of my jaw. The pain was just sitting there, waiting. Tamped down and hidden. I'd never given it a chance to leave—until now.

If my darkness wasn't quite what I'd imagined, neither was anything else. At the tail end of summer, all my constructs about everything began to swoop out of my head like a cloud of Mexican free-tailed bats (a colony flew out from under Austin's Congress Bridge every summer night at dusk, eating their own weight in mosquitos). I emptied out. I dropped all my stories about the world. What was fear? And for that matter, what was shampoo? What were cherry fudge sundaes? My head was empty.

As the pecan tree outside my studio window yellowed and undressed, I began to feel like a newborn in a twenty-five-year-old body. Suddenly, the state of being alive was neither bad nor good, but curious: what an odd thing to be born into an impermanent body! Didn't anyone else find this whole fleshy ensemble of buttocks, nostril hairs, bile ducts, and bone marrow a bit unlikely? A bit funny?

Wasn't it a little bizarre to be stuck in one of eleven billion meat bodies rushing around a 4.5-billion-year-old exploded-star planet, furiously hunting for whatever it happened to be: hot sex, fairy-tale love, the next meal, enlightenment, the down payment on a Range Rover, world peace, cell phone minutes, a house with a white picket fence, ripped abs, sanity, whatever! Wasn't it a marvel to be sentient? To be capable of love, terror, and over-the-moon joy?

Curiosity rapidly slid into wonder. Maybe I couldn't comprehend the meaning of my experience, but the fact that I was conscious at all—a point of sensory awareness—was staggering. In the mornings before work, I wandered around my studio, blinking in the sun, struck by the simplest of things. A random smattering of water droplets on the shower curtain. The juicy red igloo of a single raspberry. The Cubist masterpiece that was the geometric rip in my stocking. The burning surprise of a premature sip of tea. Small sensations sent ripples of shock through my body. I wanted to buy spray paint and tag William Wordsworth all over the walls of Austin, "The earth, and every common sight to me did seem apparell'd in celestial light!"

My riot of golden prickly pear blooms hit full culmination with the return of hunger. For the first time in years I experienced appetite. The aroma of garlic roasting in butter caused my mouth to salivate instead of caking dry with nausea. I craved chicken enchiladas with tomatillo sauce; dragon rolls topped with raw eel and orange tobiko; heaping slices of chocolate fudge cake; and round breakfast tacos filled with potatoes, salsa, and cheese. My hips and thighs began to fill out. Light returned to my eyes. The peanut butter and jelly jars gradually migrated to the back of the refrigerator. I was coming back into my body.

On January 1, 2013—six months after I hoisted the white flag of surrender—I woke before sunrise and lay still under the covers, watching the dark slowly lift into dusty gray light. No one had to tell me. Every cell in my body was already singing the news: *the dark days are over*. I was done. I was free. And not only was I free—I was more alive than before I'd fallen apart.

There had been no profound epiphany. No burning bushes or choir of triumphant angels. If I'd come to any conclusion it was simply that I was no longer interested in solving an unsolvable mystery—I was interested in living it. Meaning was not an intellectual concept that could be captured in a net, labeled, and pinned to a board. It was a physical act, a continuous investigation renewed each morning. A decision to boldly explore despite chaos and messy fragility. A choice to give myself to the world without any promise that life would make sense or end up with a neatly tied bow.

Like everyone else, I would still be confronted with a million uncertainties. I would still have to wrestle with the question of why brutal things happen to innocent people. I would still wake up with anxiety some mornings. I would still feel that reflexive craving for finite solutions and happy endings where the heroine is carted off into the horizon in a horse-drawn carriage. But certainty or no, I was finally ready to leave my cave. I was all in—even if it meant falling down, getting lost, and making a mess of things.

A little over three months later, on March 25, I logged on to OkCupid for the first time. Fifteen minutes after finishing my profile, I fired off a message to a grinning scientist in a mariachi bow tie. *Dear Tent Man, Diogenes just happens to be my favorite ancient Greek dude.*

. . .

I'm all in. That's what I told Jeff, back in Austin when he asked me to join his adventure. Over the course of our short relationship I'd metaphorically fallen down, gotten lost, and made a mess of things. But there had been a surprising literal fulfillment as well. My new credo forced me out of my head, away from the relative safety of intellectualism, and into the physicality of each moment. I literally fell when my dress caught on the guardrail outside of Budapest. I was genuinely lost from the moment we left Houston. My body had expressed itself in stickiness, dampness, and sweat—on the twenty-three-hour bus ride to Dubrovnik, at our hitchhiking site on the Croatian border, and now, once again, as we floated back down the staircases of Dubrovnik towards the deep timpani booms of the orchestra in Luža Square.

I grabbed Jeff's arm. "Not to ruin the magic of the moment, but my underwear feels weird. I think I need to find a bathroom ASAP." During our visit to the turret, my period had somehow escalated into a dire hygienic situation. This was one form of messiness Jeff would never have to worry about. Menstruation was enough to deal with at home—managing it on the road was a nightmare. For all of his minimalist gallivanting, Jeff would never be forced to run his hand over the back of his pants to make sure he hadn't bled through his only outfit. Since puberty, I'd reluctantly thrown away piles of stained clothes and sheets. My dress was at serious risk of an unwanted dye job.

"Can you make it to the square?" Jeff asked, looking concerned.

"I think so."

The music in the square was deafening. Tourists

surrounded the orchestra, smartphones raised to record the spectacle. Jeff craned his head, trying to scan the square. "Okay . . . I don't see any public bathrooms. Should we find a restaurant?"

"I . . . uh . . . don't think we have time for that."

Everything below the waist was bad going on worse. My desire to maintain basic standards of social decorum was rapidly losing ground to the desire to avoid looking like I'd been on the losing end of a street shootout. *What to do?*

I chose the fountain out of sheer desperation. The tiered Little Onofrio's Fountain was a well-known landmark half set in one of the marble alcoves of Luža Square. It was situated directly across from Saint Blaise Church, where the crowded orchestra was warming up with strains of Verdi. On top of the church, Saint Blaise himself—the patron saint of wool combers—overlooked the streams of thirsty tourists who paused at the fountain's gargoyle spouts to refill water bottles and steal a cool sip of spring water.

"I'm going to need you to run interference for me," I told Jeff.

"Why? What are you going to do?" he asked.

"Something Emily Post would *really* not approve of."

I furtively slid into the narrow, foot-wide corridor of

space between the edge of the fountain and the alcove wall. I was hardly an exhibitionist, but there was something strangely thrilling about surreptitiously changing a blood-soaked feminine pad in full view of five hundred tourists, the bearded patron saint of wool combers, and a full orchestra rehearsing Wagner's *Tristan and Isolde*.

Jeff was supposed to be standing guard by the fountain, but when I looked over he was shamelessly grinning with his phone in hand.

"You are not documenting this," I hissed.

"Trust me," he said. "You're gonna want to remember this moment."

"If you show anyone I swear I'll tell all your friends you lost your virginity on a golf course right before you got caught by her dad."

"Don't forget to mention it was midnight on the fairway of the par-five eighth hole."

"Does *nothing* embarrass you?" I said.

"Not really."

A gasp rippled through the orchestra as a few drops of late-afternoon rain splashed onto the marble floor of Luža Square. The conductor paused mid-baton wave. Chaos ensued. Within seconds the square was a flurry of violins, cellos, and French horns scattering for cover. A gang of scrawny boys wrestled a piano down a flight of steps while a motherly type followed along, snapping commands that needed no translation. *Careful! Not too fast!* It was a window of opportunity. I rolled up the soiled pad in my fist and slipped ninja-like away from the fountain.

"Mission accomplished," I said.

"Done like a true politician," said Jeff. "You wait for a moment of chaos and slide legislation through unnoticed."

. . .

We ended the night ten miles away in Cavtat, a tranquil seaside village wrapped around a crescent bay. Locals told us it was the quieter, tinier sister of Dubrovnik, but when we stepped off the bus we were faced with the same landscape of boutique hotels, upper-crust cafés, and Ralph Lauren polos. We had no place to sleep, but—for the first time—I didn't balk when Jeff suggested we just walk along the dark seafront and see what came up.

We only made it a little ways down the boardwalk when a woman stopped us. "Where are you from?" she said, staring curiously at Jeff's hat. Jeff said we were from Nigeria. She laughed and said her name was Marina. She was a Cavtat local closing up a tour shop for the night. There was no sales pitch—she just wanted company during the end of her shift. She showed us pictures of her daughter and made a couple jokes about Tito, the former Yugoslav dictator.

"Where are you staying tonight?" she asked us.

"Well, to be honest, we have no idea," said Jeff.

"Really?" she looked surprised. "My husband knows the owner of a little place just down the road. You want me to call?"

"Sure. Why not?" I said.

Marina made a call, then locked up her shop and led us further down the boardwalk to an ocean bar with rooms overhead. The room had a king-sized bed with a velvet blanket, a huge shower, and a balcony view right on the sea. It cost less than a couple movie tickets and bucket of popcorn.

"Will this work for you guys?" asked Marina.

"Oh my god, yes! This is perfect." I laughed.

"And that's how it's done," smiled Jeff.

CHAPTER 15 | The Middle Ages

We began the final leg of the journey at a white plastic table in the food court of the Dubrovnik airport. Our flight to Scotland didn't leave for another half hour so Jeff pulled out his notebook and opened it to a fresh page. We were due for another experiment evaluation. Back in our seaside room, he'd obsessively spread all our items across the bed for a final accounting. In the "gained" pile were four Hagia Sophia postcards, a handful of feminine products, a pile of assorted foreign change, and the small tube of toothpaste I insisted on picking up in Athens. In the "lost" pile was a map of the Balkans and an electrical socket adapter we'd accidentally left behind at a Budapest shisha restaurant. That was it.

"Win some, lose some," mused Jeff. "Though I've got to say, you did embrace your inner hoarder with the *four* postcards. Such extravagance."

"You better watch it," I said, punching his shoulder. "Your friends back home aren't asking how I managed to survive three weeks without baggage. They're asking how I managed to survive three weeks with *you*."

"Yeah, yeah. I'm sure they're gathering cardinal votes and petitioning the pope for your sainthood as we speak," he laughed. "But, honestly. What do you think? Hasn't it been great without any baggage?"

"You know what?" I said. "It's been amazing."

Traveling with next to nothing had gone from a frightening leap of faith to a casual afterthought. I'd grown completely accustomed to the absence of stuff by the time we reached Athens. The summery Mediterranean climate presented no challenges to our apparel and we cruised through spaces so rapidly that aside from our Couchsurfing hosts, no one was any the wiser about our one-trick wardrobe. After seven countries, eighteen days, and 1,700 miles, it appeared that the great secret to minimalist travel (at least in Turkey and Eastern Europe) could more or less be boiled down to soap and water, a solid pair of shoes, and occasional access to WiFi.

But my sense of amazement was less about surviving

the absence of backpacks and more about the magic that naturally flowed into spaces formerly occupied by possessions and plans. I was amazed at how my senses sharpened when I wasn't worried about watching my bags, or checking into a reservation on time, or hitting beats on a carefully planned itinerary. There was nothing wrong with itineraries, but it was gratifying to know that I was capable of such flexibility.

I was amazed at the liberation that came with waking up, tossing a toothbrush in a purse, and walking out the door without looking back. (Hadn't everyone felt that inner compulsion at some point in life? My mother still says that in the throes of rearing five children, she occasionally daydreamed about getting in the car and driving north on I-35 until she hit Canada, a throwback to her hitchhiking days.)

I was amazed that intentionally throwing myself at the mercy of the moment had ended not in some sort of sordid travel catastrophe, but in the sort of surreal adventure that would potentially cause future nursing home aides to up my medication and say, "There goes Ms. Bensen again—warbling on about the 'time' she traveled around the world in one dress with a scientist who lived in a dumpster."

. . .

Everyone back home had fretted that we'd develop hypothermia once we hit the chilly heaths of Scotland, but the plane landed in Edinburgh on one of the hottest days of the year. The shuttle ride from the airport to the city centre was cheery and blue—a rare sight. I'd hardly seen a dab of clear sky seven years earlier when my mother and I took a sightseeing trip from London to Inverness—a low-budget tour that celebrated both my high school graduation and a distant family history that lived on in my brother's ruddy beard, my grandmother's Steuart surname, and the crooked teeth I and all my siblings inherited.

As a teenager, I'd taken an immediate liking to the Scots. They were rowdier than the English. Scotland had a palpable underdog edge that had never been entirely subdued by crumpets and Earl Grey tea. From wild heather highlands to mirror-clear lochs, the entire Scottish landscape felt uncannily familiar the first time I saw it as a seventeen-year-old—like some memory rolling around in my DNA.

From the shuttle bus window, Edinburgh Castle looked just like I remembered it—a slightly ominous stone fortress that, from a distance, seemed to rise right out of the mound of black volcanic basalt that dominated the Edinburgh skyline. Beneath the shadow of Castle Rock, the mossy green lawns of the Princess Street Gardens were covered with a field of picnic blankets and pale sunbathers basking in the delicious swelter of the sixty-nine-degree afternoon. The entire scene seemed like a testament to one Scottish comedian's wry joke that there are two seasons in Scotland: June and winter.

Jeff's former doctoral advisor, Jamie, lived in the port district of Leith. It was a working-class neighbourhood that had once been home to the shipbuilders, fishermen, and whalers who worked along the wide estuary of Scotland's River Forth. After the Second World War, the neighbourhood earned a seedier reputation as the red light part of town, but in the 1980s the slums were replaced by a shiny new wave of homes, pubs, and restaurants only slightly reminiscent of any former grit.

"Everything's back in jolly old English," observed Jeff as we walked down a long row of grim neoclassical buildings all set with the same blocks of cinder stone, like something out of Dickens. "We speak the language, we know the city, and we've already settled on where we're staying tonight. It's almost too easy," said Jeff with genuine remorse.

He primed me on Jamie and Vicky on the way to their house.

"Jamie is pure brilliance. He's one of the youngest full pro-fessors at the University of Edinburgh and he publishes as much as some entire academic departments. He's very sharp, very quiet, and *very* British. A lot going on under the sur-face. Vicky is his wife. She's a museum curator and one of the brightest souls you could ever hope to meet." He paced down the sidewalk, excited to see his friends. "Let's see. What else? They have one baby and Uncle Jeffy might end up babysit-ting because Vicky's two weeks away from popping out the next one."

Jamie and Vicky lived on a quiet side street in a brick row house with glass-paned windows and a slate coloured door, which Jamie answered after a knock or two. He was exactly as Jeff described: the quintessential academic, tall, serious, and reserved—perhaps slightly unaccustomed to the bear hug that Jeff enveloped him in as soon as we stepped over the threshold.

"I commend you for surviving a trip with Jefferson," said Jamie dryly as he clapped Jeff on the back. (Neither Jamie nor Vicky referred to Jeff by his actual name. Jamie called him "Jefferson" in a *very* British way. Vicky referred to him as "Jeffy.")

I laughed. "Well, that's high praise coming from someone who supervised his dissertation for four years."

"Why don't we go around to the garden?" suggested Jamie. "Vicky's at a doctor's appointment now, but she'll be around later tonight."

He led us out to a backyard garden where his mother-in-law was sitting with his blond, cherubic toddler. The garden was right out of a Monet painting. A sunny table was surrounded by sweet pea vines, pink cosmos, and a leafy plum tree. Jamie set a cheese plate on the table and cracked open a few beers. "This is lovely," I sighed.

Tranquil as it was, the domestic tableaux appeared to leave Jeff slightly unsettled. His right knee vibrated as he and Jamie caught up on the last few years. Neither one had known each other as fathers. They compared notes on childbirth, the way that having a kid changed everything, and the latest academic rumblings. There was overlap, but also differences. Where Jeff was illegally sleeping on his office floor, Jamie and Vicky were cozily ensconced in a two-bedroom house with a beautiful child, a supportive mother-in-law, a steady tenured job, a cheese plate, and a white laundry line stretched across the garden. All these markers of family life were, in Jeff's eyes, reminders of the traditional mid-life he admired but chose not to pursue—a choice that both relieved him and provoked the occasional twinge of guilt. (How would Sibel be affected by his unconventional choices? Could he be an adventurer and a good father, too?)

Early in our OkCupid correspondence, he'd described the "middle," an idea loosely derived from a scene in *Almost Famous* where Lester Bangs, a veteran rock journalist played by Phillip Seymour Hoffman, sarcastically asks fifteen-year-old William Miller, an aspiring music journalist, whether he's the star of his school. William admits his classmates hate him, and Lester offers him the comforting assurance, "You'll meet them all again on their long journey to the middle."

Jeff feared the hypothetical "middle." He worried it was a complacent revving down of the engines, a gradual slide into predictability, a middle-aged plateau where risk and exploration were shelved in favor of security and stability. He didn't want to end up in the Hindu proverb Steve Jobs once quoted: "For the first thirty years of your life, you make habits. For the last thirty years of your life, your habits make you."

On the other hand, he admitted the plateau was a perfectly natural response to modern life. There were practical reasons for settling down and developing habitual grooves. Home mortgages, management positions, retirement IRAs, kids and their arm-and-a-leg college educations—none of these were particularly conducive to wild card surprises. It wasn't that he disapproved of normalcy (or gardens, or children, or cheese plates). He simply couldn't do it himself without feeling like a contortionist trying to squeeze himself into a chest.

For him, a life devoid of surprise was akin to a serious vitamin deficiency—or worse, to exile, like Napoleon's tedious (and ultimately fatal) confinement on the damp island of St. Helena. He lived for the unexpected plot twist and the abrupt turn from one road onto another. He plunged into harebrained, end-of-the-bell-curve experiments to avoid succumbing to the slightest suggestion of habit.

"You know, living in a normal house and having kids doesn't automatically exile you to the 'middle,' right?" I occasionally chided. "Lots of ordinary people hold on to curiosity even though their mail isn't delivered to a converted dumpster." Code for: *loving someone and committing to a relationship doesn't necessarily require you to change who you are.*

He agreed, but reminders of a stable, rooted life still tended to set off alarm bells. He'd left a loving marriage, a house that he shared for six years with his former wife and daughter, and he'd held a steady university job and published scads of proper academic papers. Now he was in the process of learning how to balance his urge for unbridled freedom with his responsibility to Sibel, the sweet spark whose eyes flashed with the same mischief I so often saw in his.

He loved her unequivocally and on his weekends he took every opportunity to make sure she knew it, but he didn't unequivocally identify as *dad* in the same way he didn't identify as *boyfriend* or *professor*. He was so opposed to labels that for years he'd taped black duct tape over every label he owned—including his Volvo decal, his North Face sweater, and the Patagonia backpack he fit the sum total of his possessions into. Labels of any kind were simply too close to the middle.

. . .

Jeff's uneasiness transferred to me as we sat in the garden while Jamie splashed his son in the kiddie pool. All my musings on domesticity and wedding rings could essentially be boiled down to *the future*. The future. I'd been so consumed by the intensity of our trip that I'd hardly paused long enough to consider that it was days away from ending.

Given the obvious volatility of our experiment, Jeff and I had set up auxiliary plans to be followed in the case of a blowout, a breakup, or the simple realization that we'd committed an error in judgment and couldn't stand the sight of each other. We'd each go our separate ways. No harm, no foul. But in all of our meticulous safeguarding, we'd failed to plot out what to do if we actually finished our ridiculous venture on better terms than when we'd started. We had no strategy for our return to reality. Were we a couple or was the "other" box still ticked? Was Jeff capable of a sustainable relationship amidst his Don Quixote quest for surprise? Was I looking for a serious partnership? *Jesus*, had I really quit my job?

My stomach seized up. I was dizzy with the scent of roses and sharp cheddar. The garden fences seemed to be folding in on top of me. "Would you excuse me?" I said, standing up suddenly. "I'm gonna get a little fresh air."

"You want me to come?" asked Jeff, sensing a disturbance.

"No, no," I said. "I'll be back soon."

"Well, we're not going anywhere," said Jamie drolly.

I left the garden, unsure of where to go except—as always— towards the water. Leith Walk dead-ended into the chilly

Firth of Forth, the estuary where the River Firth flowed into the North Sea. I knew that much as I charged down the pavement. From above, I must have looked like a pea green bullet shooting down the barrel-gray boulevard, past curry houses, secondhand shops, and stained glass churches.

Aside from his recent bus confession, there were signs that Jeff and I were migrating towards each other in our own careful way. In the few short weeks before our flight to Istanbul, he took me out to his family's Hill Country farm and introduced me to Sibel, his parents, and Willie, Waylon, and Biscuit, the three Texas longhorns that freely roamed the Live Oak-covered acreage. His mother's glass of chardonnay quivered slightly when I accidentally gave away our age difference, but otherwise the meet-the-parents dinner was a warm success. I was the only woman he'd brought home to the family in the two years since his separation and divorce.

I'd introduced him to my parents, too. He strolled into their Fort Worth kitchen holding an unopened bottle of top-shelf tequila in his World War II jumpsuit. "I thought you said he was a professor," whispered my mom. My younger sister Constance was home at the time. She's an ethereal green-eyed beauty with flaxen hair that almost falls to her waist—and, she keeps a war closet full of throwing stars, Japanese katanas, and Middle Eastern scimitars. "Kneel," she told Jeff in the kitchen as she solemnly unsheathed her largest sword, a six-foot replica of a *Final Fantasy* katana. He obeyed, kneeling wide-eyed on the ivory tiles as she proceeded to knight him across each shoulder.

"Welcome to the family," she said imperiously.

"I love homeschool freaks," he sighed.

. . .

By the time Leith Walk dead-ended into a cluster of industrial docks, I was newly aware of how the northern sky was fading into a down feather gray, how the sidewalk was a Pollock painting of gull scat and gum and the row houses lining the boat channels were perfectly reflected in the placid saltwater. Solvitur ambulando: *It is solved by walking.* That's what Diogenes once declared when someone posed the question of whether motion was real or not. He simply stood up and walked away, thereby proving a point as only Diogenes could. Not for the last time, I was following his lead. Walking briskly, forcing the sea air into my lungs, propelling myself from block to block. The pace pulled me back into my body.

Why the hell was I fretting over Jeff's fear of babies

and backyard gardens when we'd only known each other a handful of weeks and couldn't take a picture without five feet of space between us? What happened to gently feeling my way through the scene at hand instead of rushing to figure things out? Flowing with the moment wasn't an ingrained reflex. I was still learning. In moments of stress, I tended to regress back to my default American Protestant view that if anything was to be gotten it was only by hard work, intense competition, and relentless force.

Jeff was skilled at orienting to the reality of the present moment. It was one of his qualities I admired most. If something popped up and blew him off course, he usually just shrugged and said, "Cool! I guess we're on a new trajectory now." He was more likely to be excited by change than frightened by it. When we visited my parents in Fort Worth, I mistakenly guided him onto the wrong freeway. I fretted over my dreadful sense of direction, but he was gleeful. "No worries!" he said, "Now we get to take the scenic route!"

Jeff took his notes from the Taoist tradition of *wu wei,* literally translated as "action without action" and "effortless doing." *Wu wei* moves flexibly with the natural order of things. If one route is blocked, instead of violently forcing it open, it intuitively chooses another based on the immediate circumstances. *Wu wei* is not apathy or indifference. It's a practical tool for exploration. The pattern of raindrops, ant paths, and elephant migrations.

Wu wei is not certainty or uncertainty because it's not in the mind at all. It's a movement; an intuitive waltz that flows, but never forces; an animate state of openness that organically shifts with the crest and fall of each moment; a playful dance with the unknown that can tear up the floor in a sweaty, heart-pounding samba or slow to a somber, swaying crawl. It's not a dance of perfection. There's plenty of room for shoulder sobs, drunken sways, and failed leaps. If it comes down to it, you can collapse in a pile on the floor. The important thing is to keep one ear cocked for the rhythm—even if it's face down on the ground tapping out the downbeat with a fingernail in the dirt.

My entire relationship with Jeff was essentially a dance practice—a chance to attune to the rhythm of each moment and follow its tempo, cadence, and swing. In Jeff's terms, it was a Texas Two Step: two steps forward, one step back, but always moving, always swirling around the creaky dance floor in a blur of fiddles, dancers, and boot-tapping onlookers. There were occasional pauses, too, when the twin fiddles went silent between songs. During those pauses we'd clear the floor to wait for the next dance—unsure of whether it would be with each other or someone new.

. . .

By the time I made it back to Jamie and Vicky's garden, it was empty and the back door was locked. The neighbors saw me wandering around in the hedges. "Go help the lady," the mother told her son, a boy who looked about eight. The boy obediently escorted me around to Jamie's front door. He reminded me of the Little Prince the way he gravely led me through the garden and down the sidewalk like he was the captain of a rescue mission. "Thank you," I told him in front of Jamie's gray door.

"Yes, ma'am," he said. We looked each other in the eyes for a half a second and then he was skipping back down the sidewalk, leaving me with a tiny tug of yearning. Jeff answered the door looking genuinely worried.

"What's wrong?" I said.

"You were gone so long . . . I wasn't sure you were coming back. Did the baby scare you?"

"No," I laughed. "The baby is great. *You* scare me."

"Oh, right," he said, his face creasing into a smile. "I get that a lot."

. . .

The next morning we woke up curled against each other on a blow-up mattress in an oversized closet that had been repurposed as Jamie's office. We'd slept hard after the giant pasta dinner Vicky had insisted on preparing despite being so round she had to stretch over her belly to reach the stove. Vicky exuded warmth and hospitality, just like Jeff had said she would ("Awwwwww, Jeffy!" she cooed when she saw him). She kindly offered to let me borrow some of her clothes when, over coffee at the kitchen table, Jamie's mother-in-law gently suggested that it might be time to throw our clothes in the wash with the rest of the family laundry. They had a point. We hadn't properly washed our clothes since Budapest and we were definitely in the red zone when it came to hygiene, but the thought of going a day without our uniforms was not without some trepidation.

"I don't know," said Jeff skeptically. "Wouldn't that be cheating?"

"It's just until the clothes dry on the line," assured Vicky. "Plus you and Jamie are about the same size and I've certainly got dresses I'm not wearing at the moment." She laughed and put her hands on her belly. "I'll bring you some things to try on."

Jeff and I hardly recognized each other when we emerged from our closet dressing room. Gone were the ostentatious lobster pants and the ripped green dress. I wore one of Vicky's floral wrap dresses and a matching navy cardigan. Jeff was in a pair of Jamie's stone-coloured khakis, which he paired with a striped baby-blue polo—by far the most demure palette I'd ever witnessed him in.

"You look like a Gap commercial," I said.

"I know," he chuckled. "How are we going to keep track of each other in a crowd?"

Jamie, Jeff, and I left the house at the same time. Jamie was setting off on his morning commute to the University of Edinburgh. We were heading out for our daily wander around the city. It was a cold morning—the coldest so far. I had Vicky's cardigan but Jeff was shivering in his short-sleeved polo. "I'm going to need a sweater," he said.

To my amazement, a sweater manifested almost as soon as he uttered the words. There, right in front of us, was an abandoned gray hoodie crumpled on the end of an empty street bench. "That will do just fine," said Jeff. It was full of holes, but after a quick sniff test he pulled it over his head as

Jamie looked on, shaking his head with wry amusement.

"Jefferson, I believe your picture appears right beside the dictionary definition of 'class,'" he said.

"Hey, reduce, reuse, recycle," said Jeff. "I'll return it by sundown in the unlikely case that someone is still holding on to this treasure."

With the problem of warmth serendipitously solved, we split ways with Jamie and walked across town to the Royal Mile, the famous mile-long medieval street culminating in the entrance to Edinburgh Castle. We only made it five steps into the milling castle grounds, a dark anthill of tourists, before we looked at each other and said, "Nope." We'd both seen the castle on previous trips, but it wasn't just that—in the last three weeks we'd toured enough forts, churches, and royal residences to make a king's eyes glaze over. Jeff had begun referring to famous UNESCO sites as "ruins and shit."

We were suffering from castle fatigue. It was the same sensory saturation I'd developed the one time I visited the Louvre. After gallery upon gallery of whale-sized master-pieces, I started to feel guilty that my pool of reactions had been whittled down to "nice." My appreciation of Rembrandt's use of light in *Bathsheba at the Baths* would prob-ably have been more pronounced if the artwork had been surrounded by kindergarten finger paintings instead of every other legendary oil portrait in the world. If we were going to gape at any more world wonders, we needed to start by spending a few hours in a Chuck E. Cheese that smelled like kid sweat and stale pizza. Context was everything.

In the end, we substituted St. Andrew's Square for Chuck E. Cheese: a green patch of grass populated by corporate business types scarfing down sandwiches on lunch break. Jeff stretched out on a sunny patch of lawn; I used his shoulder as a pillow. We promptly fell asleep, a couple of unkempt tourists napping in a crowd of polished Oxfords and Burberry silk scarves. We didn't wake up until mid-afternoon.

"Looks like we had a WEE BIT O' SLEEP," yelled Jeff as we groggily sat up and looked around.

I wiped drool away from my mouth. "Is it wrong that we flew all the way from Croatia just to take a nap in the park?"

"Don't worry," said Jeff, brushing grass off his borrowed sweater. "We were just resting up for the final stop. We've saved the best for last."

CHAPTER 16 | It is Not Certain

Professor Spiegelhalter, professor of Risk at Cambridge University, set his bright-blue glasses on his knee and thoughtfully tilted his head back against the chalk-covered blackboard in his office. "What are the chances of *that*?" he said. "That's what we're trying to understand by studying coincidence."

"Can you give an example?" asked Jeff, who was holding a mug of coffee on the fuchsia love seat across from Spiegelhalter.

"Well, suppose you're trying to track down an old friend. You try the Internet with no luck. Some time later you send your printer out to be repaired and when you get it back the paper tray is filled with a few sheets of recycled paper the technician used to test the repair. One of the recycled sheets has the email address of your old friend."

"Magical," I said, from my spot beside Jeff on the love seat.

"Yes, yes, it's quite extraordinary," said Spiegelhalter, excitedly tossing his hands into the air. "But we want to use statistics to scientifically calculate just how 'magical' it actually is."

"And what's the last coincidence you personally experienced?" said Jeff, pen poised over his notebook.

"I've only got a feeble one, really," chuckled Spiegelhalter. "I'm too unobservant. But the other day I was on the train and a friend phoned me up to ask about bacon sandwiches right as I happened to be eating a bacon sandwich."

"Good one," grinned Jeff.

The appointment with Professor Spiegelhalter was the sole reason Jeff and I had tacked the U.K. onto the end of our trip. Jeff was in the preliminary stages of developing software to measure the experience of coincidence, and who better to consult than the debonair Spiegelhalter, one of the premier researchers on the subject? Never mind that he didn't live in Austin. Or North America, for that matter. Earlier that morning, we'd hugged Jamie and Vicky goodbye and caught a short flight to Luton Airport, just north of London, where, once again, Jeff gleefully rented a car—this time a Chevy Spark with a steering wheel on the right instead of the left.

"You sure you've got this opposite side of the road thing?" I said.

He looked at me with mock hurt. "You still doubt me after all we've been through, aye love?"

The moment our plane touched down at Luton Airport, Jeff had traded in a funny Scottish accent (that sounded nothing close to Scottish) for an outrageous English one. It started innocently enough—a "bloody" here and a "bollocks" there—but it escalated quickly. By the time Jeff pulled away from Luton, he was howling, "RIIIIIIIIIIIGHTY-O, LOVE!" at the top of his lungs.

"You're going to end up making an arse of yourself in front of Spiegelhalter," I warned between hysteric giggles.

He was well aware that normal Brits sounded nothing like his campy Austin Powers accent, but the knowledge did nothing to deter his enthusiasm. "RIIIIIIIIIIIGHTY-O, LOVE! Would you fancy a wee pot of PORRIDGE with your chippies?"

He was giddy right until we parked the car in front of the Isaac Newton Institute for Mathematical Sciences—named in honor of the fellow who invented calculus and developed the Laws of Motion on the Cambridge grounds. A descendant of the famous apple tree that (allegedly) cemented his theory of universal gravitation was planted nearby on the Trinity College lawn. Jeff had long admired the ambition of Newton—a troubled, withdrawn man who wanted nothing less than to solve the invisible mechanisms governing the entire universe. I too admired Newton, but more because he managed to contribute something significant to the world despite a plague of wretched mental breakdowns.

As Jeff pulled open the glass entrance door, I wondered what Newton would think of the institute that bore his name. The complex of buildings looked nothing like the distinguished, hallowed halls that Cambridge boasted about on brochures. They looked more like cylindrical UFO pods that had immigrated from some far corner of the galaxy and settled on the Cambridge field.

Architecture aside, the Cambridge mathematicians were serious. Jeff reported that the men's room was equipped with a full-size chalkboard on the off chance that brilliance struck while sitting on the pot. (If Archimedes solved buoyancy naked in a bathtub, who knew what might be solved whilst musing upon the porcelain throne?) The bathroom I stumbled into featured a full shower stocked with toiletries, shaving razors, and lavender body wash—suggesting that some scholars were so dedicated they couldn't be bothered to leave at all.

Spiegelhalter met us in a hushed cafeteria hall where the aura of calculations was so thick you could practically pull numbers out of the air. To my surprise, he looked nothing like the sort of Cambridge mathematics professor who might be caught scribbling genius on the chalkboard in the loo (distracted, powdered wig askew). Spiegelhalter had TV personality charm and a laid-back style. His hair was snow white, his eyebrows were dark, and his salt-and-pepper beard was trim—a stark contrast to Jeff's threadbare sweater and uncouth, week-old beard.

"Welcome to the institute," said Spiegelhalter, gesturing grandly around the room. "You might just see Stephen trundling about." By "Stephen" he meant Stephen Hawking, the Lucasian Chair in Mathematics (the same position Newton held almost 350 years earlier). I could feel Jeff consciously willing himself not to shout "RIIIIIIIIIIIIGHTY-O, MATE" as we followed Spiegelhalter's white shock of hair up to his office, a cozy, windowed affair with the requisite stacks of journal articles, coffee-stained mugs, and shelves of haphazardly arranged books. A small poster with a Blaise Pascal quote rested on the blackboard ledge: "It is not certain that everything is uncertain."

Jeff's meeting with Spiegelhalter was another step in his ongoing research about the connections between seemingly random intersections. The investigation was increasingly feasible given the interconnectivity of the Internet and the rapid advances of big data. Jeff wanted to know whether climbing the exact same oak tree on the exact same day could be explained by advanced statistics or if there were other scientific processes that might explain how and why we had both gravitated to the same locus in time and space.

My eyes drifted back to the Pascal quote on the blackboard as Jeff and Spiegelhalter jockeyed ideas back and forth. *It is not certain that everything is uncertain.* Maybe there were uncertainties that scientists could solve, but there were also many questions that, by their very nature, would never have a definite answer. Science could explain process and correlation, but no amount of big data or super hadron colliders could ever serve up meaning on a screen.

Over the last few years, my responses to uncertainty and suffering had run the gamut. I'd cycled from anger to disillusionment to total withdrawal. I'd sworn off the idea of "following my dreams" as a trite cliché in a world blighted by inequality, environmental destruction, corporate greed, and modern colonialism. But now, sitting in Spiegelhalter's cluttered office, I realized that in the maddening swirl of the last few months, I'd come full circle.

The world would always need dreamers: people willing to follow their inner draw and pursue the paths most conducive to creation. Dreamers, seekers, and healers are *especially* critical in the face of uncertainty and suffering. The crucial caveat that never makes it onto the inspirational "follow your dreams" prints is simple: *Follow your dreams, but let go of the outcomes.*

Yes, we must dream our big dreams and our secret desires, but dream them lightly. Follow them nimbly. Adapt, flow, and alter course as life lobs unexpected surprises in our direction. There will be occasions that require us to set old dreams down and gather new ones up. For every flourishing period of action and realization, there may also be dry periods that push us into the desert, devoid of direction. As in nature, these cycles are natural—necessary even.

If I hadn't viewed my life through the lens of a dreamer, I never would've messaged Jeff on OkCupid. I certainly wouldn't have bought a ticket to Turkey, and there's no way

I'd be sitting in a Cambridge office ruminating on the nature of coincidence.

. . .

Jeff, Spiegelhalter, and I finished the meeting at Cambridge with bacon sandwiches from the cafeteria, which we shared on the manicured lawn. Then it was off to London, our final stop. We were scheduled to meet Bigbee, another one of Jeff's college friends, who now worked as an investment analyst in the financial sector. All we had to do was drop the rental car at the Enterprise office in downtown London.

London's evening rush hour is not for the faint of heart. On the outskirts of town we pulled into a gas station to pay the $18 congestion charge fee, a tax applied to any car driving within a certain downtown radius between the hours of 7 p.m. and 10 p.m. After that, we just had to deal with daunting traffic. I'd been to London once before and had a general lay of the land. Even so, it was a mistake to volunteer myself as navigator.

"Should I turn right or left at the intersection?" asked Jeff.

"Well, that really depends on which street we're on," I said running my finger across the rental car map. "Turn left. No, no . . . hold on. Right! Dammit. We should have gone *right*. Or straight?"

"That's okay. Just tell me how to turn around."

"Ummm . . . I can't tell if this is a one-way street or . . . are we going south? Tell me if you see Big Ben. I know where that is."

"Excuse me, sir," said Jeff, shouting at a taxi driver out the window. "Can you direct me towards King Street?"

The taxi driver yelled something incoherent and shrugged his shoulders. With nothing to rely on but my inner compass, we drove down toward The Mall, around Buckingham Palace (three times), and across London Bridge to the other side of the River Thames.

"We should be getting *really* close," I nervously assured Jeff. "Except . . ."

"Except *what*?" growled Jeff. He was beginning to lose his cool.

"Except it should be Temple Avenue coming up and instead it's Weavers Lane."

"Look, can you point to the map and show me exactly where we are?"

I realized my mistake as I put my finger on the map. "Oh dear, oh dear . . ."

"What?"

"Well, I'm a bit turned around . . ."

"WOMAN. WHERE ARE WE?"

"We're on the wrong side of the Thames," I confessed, close to tears. "I was holding the map somewhat . . . upside down."

"FUCKING HELL!" Jeff's face was red. It was the first time I'd ever witnessed him lose control. And over such a mundane predicament, too. We'd fallen into the classic couples argument, replete with crumpled map and shouting tirade (all we were missing was the part where I ordered him to pull over and ask for directions). He did compose himself quickly, to his credit.

"I'm sorry," he said, breathing out through his mouth. "Let's pull over and park the car. There's nothing some fish and chips can't fix."

"Righty-o, love," I said under my breath, knowing his apology would rise up once our feet were on the ground.

. . .

By the time we finished our fish and chips and established where King Street was actually located in relation to the Thames, the Enterprise rental office had long since closed.

Jeff shrugged, back to his normal cool. *Que sera sera.* We left the car until morning and took the tube to Chelsea, where Bigbee lived. "This guy's brilliant," said Jeff on the way over. "Major nerd alert. In high school he won the state 'calculator championship' because the guy basically grew an appendage consisting of an HP32S Reverse Polish Notation scientific calculator. Now he's crunching numbers with bigger toys."

If Bigbee was a major nerd, he disguised it well. The man who opened the door and ushered us into his Chelsea apartment was clean-cut, well spoken, and had an affable, all-American air that reminded me of baseball bats and lemonade. Even his name—Bigbee—sounded like a 1950s general store or an apple varietal. He shared a small but posh flat with his wife and daughter, who were away visiting family in Turkey. It was just him and a freezer full of pre-prepared meals his wife had left sealed in plastic containers.

"Come on in, guys," he said, showing us into a living room lined with smiling pictures of family. "So, this is really it, huh?"

"Yeah, man," said Jeff. "Can you believe it? I haven't even washed my underwear once."

Bigbee chuckled and good-naturedly waved his hand.

Anyone who knew Jeff from the days when he skinny-dipped through every fountain on the Texas A&M campus knew that he tended to abide by the LBJ adage: never let the truth get in the way of a good story. In the way of old friends, both Bigbee and Jeff seemed to revert back to their younger, rowdier selves within minutes of reuniting.

"You know what?" said Bigbee, suddenly inspired to join the ranks of our devil-may-care club. "We should ride *bikes*. I've always wanted to see London by bike. Tomorrow we'll rent a couple and see where we end up."

"Sounds good," said Jeff, turning to me. "You game?"

"I'll do it as long as Bigbee navigates," I said. "Based on my recent Magellan-worthy performance, we'd aim for Buckingham Palace and end up in Belfast."

True to his word, Bigbee rented three bikes the next afternoon. He couldn't have chosen a better day to guide our biking brigade through London. It was sunny and cloudless—a consummate summer afternoon that promised nothing could go wrong. I was initially nervous about the mechanics of biking in a dress, but after a few blocks of awkwardly bent knees I gave up on modesty and let the breeze have its way with the hem of my dress (Jeff dinged his bike bell whenever he caught a gratuitous flash of thigh).

I was more concerned with avoiding the double-decker buses that lumbered perilously close to my handlebars. Jeff had no such qualms. At one point I screamed when he paused in the middle of a bus lane to strike up a conversation with a panhandler. Behind him, a double decker was pulling in so close he could've turned his head and licked the cherry red paint. "What!" said Jeff. "I had like three spare inches!"

With Jeff still intact, Bigbee took us through Hyde Park, where we happened across an open-air art installation by Sou Fujimoto. From far away it looked like a crosshatched cloud, but as we moved closer it morphed into a four-story climbable jungle gym made of glass and giant white tooth-picks. Jeff requested a side-by-side photo and then we glided on, past 221B Baker Street, where a line of literary devotees lined the sidewalk waiting to tour the fictional quarters of Sherlock Holmes.

We detoured through Regents Park, a parade of stroll-ers, soccer matches, and kids pelting breadcrumbs at ducks, and then settled in for a long eastward haul to the Shoreditch neighbourhood, an industrial haven for London's indie scene with vibrant street murals, renovated warehouses, and grungy side streets. The epic ride concluded in a grassy square filled with artists and college students. (Open-air urinals ringed the square, a visual metaphor for the sheer number of beers consumed on the premises.)

"Man!" said Bigbee contentedly. "That was *really* great. I'm seeing a whole different side of my city."

"There's something so satisfying about wandering your own streets," I smiled. "Back in Austin, Jeff and I just walk out the door and see if we can get lost. I mean the sensory thrill is obviously heightened when we drop into a place where everything is unfamiliar—that's why we chose to go on this trip—but there's so much right in front of us, too."

Jeff chimed in, "Yeah, it's easy to get stuck in your own little world—like, to live in a big city with hundreds of restaurants, but to order the same thing at the same three restaurants over and over."

"That's true," Bigbee said. "It's easy to get complacent. You stop noticing your environment if you don't actively look."

I nodded. "Exactly. And I never want to lose that curiosity. There are always strangers I've never talked to and streets I've never noticed. Plants changing with the seasons. Neighbors sitting out on their porches. The magic of exploration doesn't *only* show up when I jump on a international flight."

"Yep," said Jeff. "We can do it next to Shoreditch. We can do it at home."

. . .

The promise of home appeared slightly sooner than I'd expected. The next morning Jeff opened the bathroom door and charged into Bigbee's spare room holding a towel around his waist, still dripping from the shower. His eyes were wild.

"How long will it take you to get packed?" he asked breathlessly.

"Is that supposed to be a joke?" I said.

"There's a Heathrow flight back to Houston that leaves today instead of tomorrow. The only problem is that it takes off in less than two hours. You wanna make a run for it?"

I laughed, "Sure, I guess? But will Bigbee mind?"

We'd already discussed going home a little earlier. I was overstimulated to the point that if faced with the decision, I'd have chosen a dank monk's cell over a private tour of Buckingham Palace guided by the queen. Jeff, on the other hand, was fidgety. Our adventure was coming to a close and the tranquil comfort of Bigbee's flat lent itself a little too well to contemplation *(What did all this mean? What would happen when the plane landed in Austin?)*. A mad dash to the airport was his way of keeping the momentum rolling. *No time for navel gazing! On we go!*

His towel zipped down the hallway into the kitchen, where Bigbee was loading the dishwasher. "Bigbee! How long does it take to get to Heathrow from here?"

"I don't know, man," I heard Bigbee say, sounding taken aback. "I guess the fastest thing would be to take a taxi to the Earl's Court station and then take the tube from there. You might be able to make it in under an hour."

Jeff was silent, probably calculating something on his phone. I could hear the clink of glasses in the sink. And then Jeff again: "Sorry to leave without warning, brother, but there's been a change in plans. Clara and I are going to make a mad dash for the airport."

Bigbee was surprised. "Oh really? Is everything okay?"

"We're all good," said Jeff. "I just woke up with this crazy urge to get back to work. I've got all these serious projects to attend to—you know, like fitting a house into a dumpster."

Bigbee seemed a bit sad to lose the company, but he rallied, "Why not? I'll call you guys a cab."

The rush felt good. I reached for the emerald dress and slid my arms into it. It would be the last time I ran my finger over each button from hem to collar. I would never wear the dress again, of that I was certain. Renegade green threads were escaping from seams like slender stems of grass. The gash from the guardrail was even further frayed. But even if the dress had been in pristine shape it would still be the last time. My travel uniform was forever linked to these twenty-one days; to every border, road, and sky; to greasy buses and rocking trains; to folding couches, bars of borrowed soap, and cups of Turkish tea; to new friends and generous strangers; to an unexpected connection that felt a lot like love.

Home was waiting with a closet full of dresses and yet I was struck by the newfound desire to return and purge my apartment of every item that didn't fall under the categories of "joy" or "practical use." Once a baseline for wellbeing was met, a comfortable existence wasn't necessarily an accessorized one. In our experiment, the marker for success was not a groundbreaking revelation about consumption or a preachy sermon about the ills of Black Friday. Rather, it was the simple acknowledgement that, after the initial jump, we'd mostly forgotten we were performing an experiment at all.

The tube of Greek toothpaste was the last item I tucked into my purse before clicking the clasp shut. We were out the door and in the taxi in less than ten minutes—a new record.

"Is nothing ever straightforward with you?" I yelled, rushing to keep up with Jeff's long red legs as we skipped down the stairs into the Earl's Court station. The station was packed with weekend tourists shouldering for tickets. Jeff replied to my comment with a happy cackle.

"Okay, we need to be strategic. Can you stand in that line? I'll stand in this one. Whoever gets to the counter first buys the tickets," he said. "We're *going* to make it to Heathrow and hop our asses on that plane."

And we did. We checked into our Heathrow gate with half an hour to spare. But it was only after finding our seats on the 767 that the weight of departure began to sink in.

"Oh my god, we're going home," I said.

"Can you believe it?" said Jeff. "This whole trip doesn't even seem real." He took out his notebook and began flipping through pages he'd taped full of ticket stubs, scrawled directions, WiFi passcodes, Hungarian phrases, and Couchsurfing numbers. On one of the pages I'd carefully printed out the Turkish phrase for "I love you" when he wasn't looking. *Seni seviyorum.* I couldn't say it to his face, but at some point he'd thumb back through the pages and find my handwriting along the edge. A tiny surprise. Or maybe he wouldn't be surprised. He liked to remind me that I had no poker face. Everything slipped out through my eyes.

"Wonder what's going to happen next?" I said. It was a rhetorical question. I already knew his answer. And of course, he obliged.

"We'll see. We'll see."

He said the words tenderly, like he was looking out towards a horizon where something was waiting. I took his hand in mine and we held each other tight. Very tight. I could feel the blood pumping through our wrists. *Ba-DUM. Ba-DUM. Ba-DUM.* There was the rhythm again, suffused in every moment. All I had to do was follow its lead. I wasn't afraid of being lost anymore.

Epilogue

I write these closing words on a bus surrounded by snow-capped mountains 4 degrees of latitude north of the Arctic Circle. It seemed appropriate to end the story the same way it began: diving into the world with nothing but a small purse and a single dress when I could be doing something far more practical.

This journey through the ethereal white tundra is the fourth No Baggage installation (full disclosure: I do have a small briefcase holding my laptop and manuscript notes). Jeff is sitting across from me on the bus, wearing the same unwashed Levi's jeans he put on a week ago. We're both wearing long underwear, handwashed in arctic tap water.

It's been exactly two years since I met him on the steps of the Texas Capitol. Since then we've had the privilege of crossing rope bridges in the Amazon jungle, watching the sun rise above Mesopotamia on a Turkish mountain top, and touring one of Stalin's largest Soviet steel plants in the Republic of Georgia while gleefully (and seriously) pretending to be World Trade Organization consultants. With each trip, we challenge ourselves to be more thoughtful and ethical travelers.

Some things have changed dramatically. Jeff and I refer to each other as boyfriend/girlfriend without turning pale. Our relationship has taken on much more structure and definition. We make occasional plans in advance. We are openly tender towards each other and write notes that include the words "I love you."

Other things haven't changed at all. After two years. I still feel a jolt of happiness when I look up and see Jeff walking into the room. Far from being a one-off, our experimental streak continues. (True to his word, Jeff recently finished up a year of living in a used dumpster. His daughter helped him paint it.) We still wander the streets of our city. We still have no idea where all of this is leading.

The final aspect that has shifted is my willingness to speak openly about mental health. I used to go to great lengths to hide my history with debilitating anxiety. In the

United States, it's often safer to suffer in silence than to admit to struggling with a psychological or emotional disorder. In that culture of silence I assumed I was a freak mutation. Now I know—from countless frank conversations—that it would be hard to find someone who *hasn't* struggled with depression, grief, PTSD, anxiety, or an eating disorder.

Though I no longer feel timid about addressing mental illness, I do admit to feeling a little shy about sharing the story of what is essentially a sensitive college graduate crumbling psychologically under the realization that the real world can be a fragile and unforgiving place—a reality that is glaringly obvious for so many on this planet. I do share it because reckoning with uncertainty is something that none of us can escape. Not everyone will internalize the experience of uncertainty quite as intensely as I did or attempt to face it with such an outrageous experiment, but I will be glad I documented my journey if even one reader feels a little less alone as they navigate the fragile, messy brilliance that is life.

KE 01.17

Acknowledgments

This story was a surprise in every sense of the word. When the chance to tell it arose, I sat down in front of my laptop and tremblingly typed "how to write a book" in the search tab. Since then I've relied on a fantastic group of supporters, without whom, this book would not exist. Thanks to my agent, Stacy Testa, who enthusiastically championed the story from the very start. Thanks to Jennifer Kasius, my tireless yet calm editor, and all the staff at Running Press who have invested so much thought, time, and energy into this book. Thanks to Abe Louise Young, Katie Matlack, Anna Yarrow, and Sarah Bensen for their generous feedback and critique. Thanks to the entire Bensen tribe for their consistent and loving support. And finally, thanks to Jeff Wilson, who instigated this baggage-less adventure in the first place and has remained an incredible partner and friend through all of the strange and surprising events that followed it.